Cambridge El

GW00982536

Elements in Prag
edited by
Jonathan Culpeper
Lancaster University, UK
Michael Haugh
University of Queensland, Australia

THE DARK MATTER
OF PRAGMATICS

Known Unknowns

Stephen C. Levinson
Max Planck Institute for Psycholinguistics

CAMBRIDGE
UNIVERSITY PRESS

Shaftesbury Road, Cambridge CB2 8EA, United Kingdom

One Liberty Plaza, 20th Floor, New York, NY 10006, USA

477 Williamstown Road, Port Melbourne, VIC 3207, Australia

314–321, 3rd Floor, Plot 3, Splendor Forum, Jasola District Centre,
New Delhi – 110025, India

103 Penang Road, #05–06/07, Visioncrest Commercial, Singapore 238467

Cambridge University Press is part of Cambridge University Press & Assessment,
a department of the University of Cambridge.

We share the University's mission to contribute to society through the pursuit of
education, learning and research at the highest international levels of excellence.

www.cambridge.org
Information on this title: www.cambridge.org/9781009489591

DOI: 10.1017/9781009489584

First published 2024

A catalogue record for this publication is available from the British Library.

ISBN 978-1-009-48959-1 Hardback
ISBN 978-1-009-48963-8 Paperback
ISSN 2633-6464 (online)
ISSN 2633-6456 (print)

The Dark Matter of Pragmatics

Known Unknowns

Elements in Pragmatics

DOI: 10.1017/9781009489584
First published online: March 2024

Stephen C. Levinson
Max Planck Institute for Psycholinguistics
Author for correspondence: Stephen C. Levinson, levinson@mpi.nl

Abstract: This Element tries to discern the known unknowns in the field of pragmatics, the 'Dark Matter' of the title. We can identify a key bottleneck in human communication, the sheer limitation on the speed of speech encoding: pragmatics occupies the niche nestled between slow speech encoding and fast comprehension. Pragmatic strategies are tricks for evading this tight encoding bottleneck by meaning more than you say. Five such tricks are reviewed, which are all domains where we have made considerable progress. We can then ask for each of these areas, where have we neglected to push the frontier forward? These are the known unknowns of pragmatics, key areas, and topics for future research. The Element thus offers a brief review of some central areas of pragmatics, and a survey of targets for future research. This title is also available as Open Access on Cambridge Core.

Keywords: pragmatics, implicit meaning, information theory, communication, language

ISBNs: 9781009489591 (HB), 9781009489638 (PB), 9781009489584 (OC)
ISSNs: 2633-6464 (online), 2633-6456 (print)

Contents

The Dark Matter of Pragmatics

Known Unknowns

Elements in Pragmatics

DOI: 10.1017/9781009489584
First published online: March 2024

Stephen C. Levinson
Max Planck Institute for Psycholinguistics
Author for correspondence: Stephen C. Levinson, levinson@mpi.nl

Abstract: This Element tries to discern the known unknowns in the field of pragmatics, the 'Dark Matter' of the title. We can identify a key bottleneck in human communication, the sheer limitation on the speed of speech encoding: pragmatics occupies the niche nestled between slow speech encoding and fast comprehension. Pragmatic strategies are tricks for evading this tight encoding bottleneck by meaning more than you say. Five such tricks are reviewed, which are all domains where we have made considerable progress. We can then ask for each of these areas, where have we neglected to push the frontier forward? These are the known unknowns of pragmatics, key areas, and topics for future research. The Element thus offers a brief review of some central areas of pragmatics, and a survey of targets for future research. This title is also available as Open Access on Cambridge Core.

Keywords: pragmatics, implicit meaning, information theory, communication, language

ISBNs: 9781009489591 (HB), 9781009489638 (PB), 9781009489584 (OC)
ISSNs: 2633-6464 (online), 2633-6456 (print)

Contents

Image shows galaxy cluster CL0025+1654 with inferred Dark Matter
in blue. Credit: J.-P. Kneib (Observatoire Midi-Pyrenees, Caltech) et al., ESA,
NASA (https://apod.nasa.gov/apod/ap030814.html)

Preface

This Element is based on a plenary lecture to the International Pragmatics Conference in Brussels in July 2023. The reception was enthusiastic enough that I thought it might be useful to write it up. The purpose of the lecture, and thus this book, was to knock the complacency out of us by drawing attention to all the things in the field of pragmatics we still don't know or only have a feeble grasp of. It was also intended as a pep-talk for our younger colleagues, to remind them actually how practically important our subject matter is. To try to get a handle on the things we don't yet know but can at least glimpse the edges of, the Element does a quick and very superficial zip through the well-developed fields of pragmatics. The book potentially has two uses. First, and its main intended use, is to help researchers in the field find lush new pastures for study. PhD students or their supervisors might therefore find it handy as an initial thing to read. There is a danger here: the author is not a spring chicken, and so much research has accumulated in many of the domains reviewed that it is very possible that I will suggest such-and-such is under-researched and be ignorant of some rather substantial recent body of work.

A second possible use is for students new to the field of pragmatics who want such an unbuttoned, whirlwind tour of what pragmatics is all about. But here there is another danger: this survey of what we know is so brief, sketchy and loose that it may give the acolyte the mistaken impression that what we do know is self-evident, imprecise and paltry compared to what we don't know! That is best countered by having in the other hand one of the thorough textbooks now available (e.g. in chronological order, Levinson 1983; Huang 2007; Senft 2014; Clift 2016). The novice will then find that pragmatics is a well-developed field of study, with a range of quite technical and advanced nooks. With that antidote, I think this book may prove useful.

One further caveat. Like the major traditions in linguistics, this work takes language spoken in verbal interaction as the basic target. There are other channels like that involved in sign languages, and many other kinds of language use, both spoken and written. All these are worthy targets of research.[1] But I start with the prejudice that it is spoken language that kickstarted the human species and is still the predominant form of language use today. So it has a special call on our attention.

1 What Is Pragmatics and Why Does It Matter?

Pragmatics is the study of how language is used to communicate. A huge amount of thinking and research over centuries has gone into the study of language,

---

[1] See, for example, Hoffmann and Bublitz 2017 on social media. Historical pragmatics is an important subdiscipline that relies of course on written texts, see e.g. Jucker and Taavitsainen 2010.

mostly into how languages are structured and how history has shaped them. Until relatively recently (the last fifty years), comparatively little had been done on systematic studies of language use. This is odd: it would be curious to study the structure of a spade or a hammer without asking what it was used for and how it was shaped for those purposes. The main reason for this relative neglect of language use is presumably simply that language is so much the central human medium – the water in which we swim – that we take the usage patterns for granted. A contributing factor is undoubtedly that until the invention of practical recording techniques, 'freezing' language usage for inspection was problematic.

But despite earlier neglect, in the last half century research in pragmatics has flourished. This Element can serve as an introduction to this vibrant field, for it will sketch many of the major developments and achievements in this domain (and by 'sketch' I mean that this is a fast and loose rendition, without any of the precision that can and has been brought to bear on the subject). But its main purpose lies beyond that, namely to identify what remains mysterious and little understood about how we communicate with language, and in this way to help direct research efforts into the future.

Why is this field important? Consider the following accident. In 1990, Avianca Flight 052 approached John F. Kennedy airport, New York, low in fuel. It was put into three holding patterns until the fuel level was critical, finally missing the runway and crashing into a hillside on Long Island with the loss of seventy-three lives. There had been repeated communications between the cockpit and the control tower, with the co-pilot repeatedly mentioning that they needed priority and were running out of fuel. But the crew failed to use the word 'emergency', which is the fixed expression along with 'mayday, mayday', to request priority landing rights. Because this fixed form was not used, the control tower assumed the situation was not critical. The assumption was based on a normal rule of thumb governing language use – if someone doesn't use the extreme end of a scale, they do not intend it, so for example saying 'The crucible is still warm' suggests it is not still red hot (see Section 7). Or consider another case. Edward aged three was delayed in language abilities, and the medics diagnosed him as autistic, which put him into specialist nurseries and schools. It turned out to be a complete misdiagnosis. Edward was largely deaf. Once that was recognized, and he was fitted with hearing aids, he could fully participate in normal school.[2] Autism in fact has a very clear pragmatic profile in social interaction, with delays and disconnectedness in response and distinctive gaze patterns. Understanding the pragmatic profile is crucial and

---

[2] www.ndcs.org.uk/information-and-support/parenting-and-family-life/families-magazine/your-stories/primary-years-stories/edwards-misdiagnosis/

would aid early diagnosis. Still not convinced about the importance of pragmatics? Then consider this too. There are sustained efforts to make AI devices interact with us, and people with physical hindrances can come to rely on them. But these systems – Alexa, Google Assistant or the more sophisticated systems too – have no competence to cope with mishearings or incomprehension, whereas real language users have multiple systems for correcting, rephrasing and compensating. AI systems desperately need a human-oriented pragmatics.

Perhaps these illustrations of the importance of the field will seem rather marginal. Well, then, consider the case of the child learning her first language. Noises are being made around her. How should the child realize that these are communicative? Mum makes noises to the child, the child smiles back, the mother laughs, and the two are engaged from early days in an exchange. The child brings to all this some kind of knowledge or instinct about communicative interaction, and it is this presumption of meaningfulness that makes it possible for the child to learn a language. In doing so, the child uses many presumptions about the use of language – for example, that it is exchanged in turns in a kind of 'proto-conversation'. These are the pragmatic foundations for language, without which all the rich resources of the full tongues cannot be mastered.

Our knowledge of pragmatics is now extensive and based on a growing body of work that extends over fifty years. Good reviews can be found in Levinson 1983; Huang 2007; Clift 2016, to mention just a few. But the main purpose of this book is to first glance at what we know, but then look beyond that, to what we do not yet understand, and so try and discern targets for future research.

2 How to Find out What We Don't Know We Don't Know

Dark Matter makes up 85 per cent of the mass of the universe, but it is invisible to current astronomical methods. We know it must exist only because of the gravitational effects it exerts on the heavenly bodies we can see. If despite thousands of years of careful observation of the heavens, we only understand at most 15 per cent of what moves the celestial bodies, then we can be fairly confident that in the short lifetime of the scientific study of pragmatics we understand rather less than that. The rest is the 'Pragmatic Dark Matter' of my title. Much of our mental life is hidden from view: we do not know, for example, how we mentally decide what to say and how to say it. We do not know why we dream, or where bursts of inspiration come from. In the same way we don't understand many aspects of how we come to construe particular utterances in the way we do in a specific context.

There are a number of specific reasons to think there is actually a lot of pragmatic Dark Matter. First, as mentioned, the subject is scarcely half a century old. Secondly, a great deal of the theory that we rely upon dates back to the foundational period, roughly 1960–1985, with forbears in the 1950s (Wittgenstein, Bar-Hillel, Carnap, Bühler and others). Early in that period the philosopher Austin (1962) introduced the notion of speech act (later systematized by Searle 1969); Grice (1967) introduced the notion of conversational implicature building on his earlier intentional theory of meaning (Grice 1957); Schegloff & Sacks (1973) introduced the principles of conversation analysis, Stalnaker (1974) building on earlier work by Strawson (1950) tried to firm up the notion of presupposition, and Fillmore (1971) systematized what we then knew about deixis. A great deal of further analysis and reanalysis quickly followed (e.g. Horn 1972; Levinson 1983; Sperber & Wilson 1986). These insights still form the core of our theoretical apparatus in pragmatics, but it is getting quite old and is surely ready for a refresh.

A third reason to suspect that we have hardly begun our explorations of language usage is that most of this theory derives from Western philosophy, and inevitably reflects the foci and preoccupations of Western scholars and societies, that is, the cultures of the Global North. Indigenous theory from elsewhere, and particularly from Asia where there are long traditions of metalinguistic thinking, would help to correct this viewpoint.[3] A fourth and related point is that pragmatic theory and analysis is very much focussed on familiar major languages, and indeed largely on European ones and English in particular. We have systematic information about the use of only perhaps 5 per cent of the world's languages (a good third of languages don't even have any grammatical descriptions; Skirgård et al. 2023). But there are some 7,000 languages spoken or signed on the planet, each with their own peculiarities, and information about their usage will certainly lead to new insights and fresh theory.

A fifth reason to think there is still much to discover is that much of the work done in pragmatics has been done with relatively unsophisticated tools, more akin to the astrophysics of Galileo or Newton than the modern world of space telescopes. But new tools and methods are increasingly becoming available. Digital video on personal computers only became available in the 1990s, making possible annotated video for the first time around 2000. It is only very recently that we have large multimodal corpora online and the facility to readily script search procedures, using for example machine learning to find the target phenomena. Recordings with multiple cameras, multiple sound channels, and time-aligned simultaneous recordings of eye-movement, ultrasound recordings of the vocal tract, heart-rate, breathing and other channels are now available.

---

[3] See for example Hanks et al. 2019.

Then there are all the resources of neuroimaging, from EEG, MEG to MRI to investigate. All these new tools and methods will throw up new phenomena we had little idea even existed.

A sixth reason to think there's a great deal still to discover is that there are still many under-developed topics of research – for example, the pragmatics of sign languages, newly described pragmatic disorders and how to improve language use of artificial agents. Interesting questions like whether pragmatic routines (like gesture repertoires, prosodic patterns, address usage) cross language-boundaries within so-called 'language areas' (e.g. the Indian subcontinent, or Meso-America) have hardly even been raised.

It is an interesting conundrum to wonder how we can convert *unknown unknowns* – that is, things we have no inklings about whatsoever – into *known unknowns*, that is, Dark Matter. In the case of astrophysics, it is by mathematically discerning the hidden forces that must account for the celestial observations. In the study of language usage one thing we can do is traverse the *known knowns*, the things we think we understand, and see just where these bump up against the edges of our known universe. That will give us a clue to what must lie just beyond our known boundaries, the known unknowns to which we should be directing our attention in the future. So, to explore these edges, this little book will take us for a wild romp through the known knowns of pragmatics in search of the known unknowns. Fasten your safety belts please!

3 The Human Communication Bottleneck and the Niche for Pragmatics

There is one necessary preliminary. Human communication is a miracle. There is nothing else like it on the planet. We are the only animals that can communicate thoughts of arbitrary complexity to each other. In this context, it might seem churlish to point to a major flaw in the design, as it were. But there is one. The fly in the ointment is a tight bottleneck on speech production. There's a physiological maximum of about seven to eight syllables per second (Laver 1994). The reasons for this are numerous. Over one hundred muscles are involved in speech production, breathing needs to be coordinated, decisions have to be made about what to say and how to say it, lexical items need retrieving, the words need to be tied together within a grammatical frame, the whole has to be phonologically encoded and finally articulated (Levelt 1989).

To get a perspective on this slow speech encoding process it is useful to convert the measure into the universal language of data transmission, namely 'bits'. Using the information theory devised by Shannon and Weaver (1949), we can calculate a maximal language data transmission speed of 96 bits per second (bps) for English (following Laver's syllable rate above).[4] If potential transmission speed is near to 100 bps, actual trends measured across numerous languages are nearer to 39 bps (Coupé et al. 2019). Now if you compare that to your typical broadband speed of 30,000,000 bps or higher one gets an interesting perspective on the speed of human language production: it is brutally slow! Psycholinguists have also ingeniously measured exactly what part of the encoding process takes how long – the standard figure is that retrieving and saying a single word will take well over half a second before anything comes out of your mouth (Levelt 1989; see Section 10).

Such slow data transmission speeds are counter-intuitive: the phenomenology is of fast and furious conversational exchange, and certainly not of plodding effort. But these facts are firm. It is important to note though that bit rates measure data transmission (coded sequences) measured in inverse probability of occurrence, not in the amounts of semantic content transferred (Floridi 2010). Semantic information is much harder to measure, and just about the only useful measure we have is Carnap & Bar-Hillel's 1952 theory of semantic information, which shares the inverse rule (information content increases inversely to probability). A useful way to think about this is that an assertion is semantically informative to the extent that it rules out states of affairs. So 'All men are mortal' is more informative than 'Englishmen are mortal'.

Now, it is quite easy to show that semantic information can be transferred much faster than we can actually speak: if you take a tape or recording of fast speech and speed it up three times you can easily understand it, and you will likely understand it even at four times the maximal speaking rate.[5] That shows that the bottleneck is a coding bottleneck, not a limit on comprehension. This gap between the coding rate and the comprehension rate is of fundamental importance for our subject. For this is *the pragmatic niche*, the zone that can be filled by ancillary means of communication. The rest of this Element is about how pragmatics fills this gap between frustratingly slow production and fast comprehension.

Now, one response to all this may be that human communication is not really characterized by supreme efficiency – people chat, lament the weather and express their social relationships in an extravagant use of banter. Yes, but that is not the point. Language use tends to optimal efficiency even when engaged in the practice of bullshit (Frankfurt 2005). Those playing golf or tennis are complete time wasters, but they are also trying to win efficiently. Just as wanderers through a park tend to make a path by taking the shortest route between two points, so

---

[4] The details of the calculation can be found in Levinson (2000: 382 n. 18 & n. 19).
[5] See e.g. Laver 1994:543, Gransier et al 2023.

words tend to shorten according to how often they are used (Zipf 1949). Humans are optimizers in communication as in everywhere else.

4 A Design Perspective on Human Communication

It is sometimes very useful to adopt a design perspective when thinking about any human or animal capacity: what would it take to retro-engineer the system under study? So let us suppose we were trying to build a language with maximal expressive or communicative effectiveness. Let us appoint an engineer to help us. Obviously, our engineer would try and maximize the data transmission rate. In the Shannon–Weaver model of communication sketched in Figure 1, the effective bit rate depends on the noise in the channel and on the construction of the language.

Noise is best countered by building in a certain amount of redundancy, and languages do this in multiple ways, for example by multiple marking of such grammatical categories as plural, as in '**Women are** the best **writers**'. The bit rate can be increased by increasing the number of phonemes and the total possible syllables – recollect that data transmission in bits is inversely related to probability of occurrence, so the rarer the segment or syllable the more 'informative' in this data transmission sense. But too many phonemes and too many syllables makes a language hard to learn and slow to speak, so in practice it's best to just pick a median figure that will give us an average 40 bps speed (Coupé et al. 2019). Incidentally, one might wonder if sign languages are constrained in the same way: although manual signs are slower to produce than spoken syllables because the articulators are much larger, this may be compensated for by the two hands and facial gestures allowing simultaneous broadcast of signals (Wilbur 2009). Given that simultaneous interpretation of sign languages to spoken languages and vice versa appears to operate at near equal speeds, we can presume that sign language encoding has roughly the same bit rate as speech (see also Grosjean 1979).

So, if the bit rate is fixed, the next thing we and our engineer will worry about is making sure we can maximize semantic informativeness, and here using the

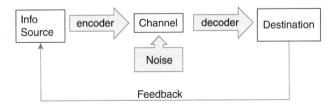

Figure 1 The Shannon–Weaver (1949) model of communication/ data transfer.

Carnap and Bar-Hillel metric (informativeness in proportion to excluded possibilities) we need to ensure that the language is capable of general statements that rule out the most possible states of affairs. So we need a lot of very broad, semantically general words, like 'person', 'thing', 'tree' and so forth, and we need quantification and negation so we can say, for example 'No women are immortal either' or 'There has never been a five-legged animal'. In short, we'll need the full apparatus that natural languages have to express logical relations using a general vocabulary.

Having done his or her best to maximize the bit-rate and the expressive potential, the next thing the engineer wants to do is somehow get around that slow speech production rate. It is frustrating that, as mentioned in section 3, numerous experiments show that we can understand much faster than we can transmit. So what the engineer will try and do is devise some ways to get around that bottleneck. His or her job is to find some tricks that will amplify the content without, alas, being able to speed up the transmission.

If our engineer is any good, he or she will come up with at least five tricks – devices to circumvent that speech production bottleneck and utilize the full potential of the gap between slow speech and fast comprehension. The rest of this Element will explore these five tricks. Each of them, it turns out, is a rich domain of pragmatics, already partially explored. So, in examining them in the following sections, we will be traversing the *known knowns* of pragmatics, in search of the edges of our knowledge, the discernible *known unknowns*, the targets for future research. For each trick to circumvent the bottleneck, we'll first describe what we know, and then turn to what these aspects indicate that we do not yet fully understand.

5 The First Trick to Circumvent the Bottleneck: Multiplying Channels

5.1 The Known Knowns: Multimodality

The first trick is a no-brainer. We have a strict coding speed limit on the speech channel. Very well, we'll use other channels as ancillary devices, for example gesture. All natural languages used in social interaction use multiple channels. For example, I can say 'He went that way' indicating leftwards with my hand. Or I can say 'The boss says redo it' while rolling my eyes, indicating disaffiliation with the message. Sometimes these different channels work to give the desirable redundancy (I say 'He turned left' while gesturing left), but more often they add new information. How many distinct channels or conduits of information are there actually?

Here we should pause to distinguish *the channel*, for example vocal-auditory vs. gestural-visual, from the *medium*, for example English vs. Swahili. English can be delivered in the visual channel by writing of course, or it can be finger spelled in sign language, hence the need for the distinction (Lyons 1977: Chapter 3). But that won't be sufficient. We also need a notion of layering. Layering of one sort is a notion familiar to linguists through for example the distinct levels of phonetics and phonology, where elements of one layer constitute elements of another. But here we need a notion of *overlayering*, that is, the possibility of a layer carrying an independent (non-constitutive) signal. A contrastive prosody can be overlaid onto the segmental signal to indicate both grammatical (e.g. interrogative) functions and attitudinal ones (Ladd 2014). Part of this has been described as *paralanguage*, for example the use of creaky voice, the relaxed vocal chords associated with self-confidence. Voice quality, amplitude, pitch and timbre can all be used in this way to add essential information to an utterance.

In a similar way we can view the gestural-visual channel as layered. I can gaze at you with narrowed or wide-open eyes, momentarily or in a sustained manner, with blinks or without blinks. A hand gesture to the left can be close to the body or extended, made with a loose hand or an index finger, and so forth. Each layer carries potentially independent meaning. As Abercrombie (1968: 55) put it, 'We speak with our vocal organs, but we converse with our entire bodies'.

So here is a way that our engineer can get around the coding bottleneck, by multiplying channels and within channels by multiplying layers. Given the number of potential channels and layers (some sketched in Figure 2) one can see that this can easily multiply the bit rate, the transmission speed, of human communication. Ray Birdwhistell, who invented the term kinesics for the study of bodily posture, estimated that at most a third of the content of human communication is verbalized.[6] That measure is suspect, but there is no doubt that the use of multiple channels can amplify and sometimes multiply the content of the spoken channel.

The study of all this is not new. The Greek and Roman orators already classified gestures, but systematic study began in the second half of the twentieth century, on the one hand by anthropologists interested in gesture and bodily deportment and on the other hand by phoneticians interested in the layering of the verbal signal. In addition, social psychologists got increasingly interested in non-verbal communication. A long-running project on the '*Natural history of an interview*' involved many of the crucial pioneers in the non-vocal channels, including Birdwhistell, Hall, Kendon, Condon, Erikson, Bateson and others,

---

[6] McDermott, R. 1980. Profile: Ray L. Birdwhistell. *The Kinesis Report*, 2(3): 1–16 (cited in Wikipedia article 'Kinesics', https://en.wikipedia.org/wiki/Kinesics#cite_note-7)

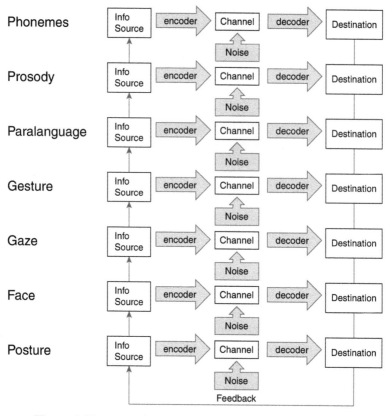

Figure 2 Circumventing the coding bottleneck by multiplying channels and layers. *The figure is only illustrative – how many channels are there actually?*

who developed the first ways of describing and annotating filmed interaction.[7] These early scholars were mavericks outside of mainstream disciplines, but with videotape and then digitized video, and from about 2000 with the birth of digital video annotators like ELAN,[8] the study of the multi-layered nature of human communication has developed very rapidly. Recent technical progress is beginning to make it possible, using machine learning, to automatically retrieve facial expressions and particular gestures.

Pragmatics has embraced all these developments, under the rubric of 'multi-modality', and the study of manual gesture in particular is well advanced. There are standard ways of breaking down hand movements, for example, into preparation phases, the stroke or main gesture, its potential hold, and then retraction (Kita et al. 1998). Interestingly, gestures seem to be integrated into

---

[7] See https://www.lib.uchicago.edu/mca/mca-15-098.pdf   [8] https://archive.mpi.nl/tla/elan

comprehension at the same speed as the words that accompany them (Özyurek 2014). Sign languages are particularly pertinent with regard to overlayering because of the ability to simultaneously layer multiple articulators both according to grammatical or linguistic rules and according to expressive needs – the face for example plays a critical role in addition to the two hands (Loos et al. 2022).

To sum up, much progress has been made in showing how multimodality compensates for the tight bottleneck on speech production. However, even a cursory review of what we already know throws up many unanswered questions, the Dark Matter that we are after.

5.2 The Corresponding Dark Matter: An Orchestra with 150 Instruments

The study of multimodal communication is relatively new, dependant as it has been on the innovation of recording technologies. So there is plenty we do not know, and some of the known unknowns are obvious. First, manual gestures have been highly studied, but all the other channels and layers lag far behind. The face has been particularly neglected, except in sign language where it sometimes plays a grammatical role (marking e.g. conditionals or questions) and where a lexical item may require a particular expression. But the role of the face in spoken interaction remains very underexplored. On the face alone many potentially co-occurring layers are possible: forehead (frontalis muscle), individual eyebrows, mouth, teeth and jaw position, head tilt and movement in three dimensions, and gaze. Darwin (1872) advanced the idea that facial expressions may have an innate basis, a view taken to extremes by Ekman et al. (1972), but it is well known that communicative facial expressions are also culturally shaped (Russell 1995). Japanese tend to look to the eyes in situations where Americans look to the mouth, and I have worked in a Papuan culture where wrinkling the nose is not as predicted by Ekman associated with disgust but is rather an expression of 'Wow!' Most investigations of facial expressions have used still photos, while what the pragmaticist is interested in is fleeting expressions in social interaction, not adequately captured in stills.

So the situation is this: we have no idea how many layers or channels are reliably in use across cultures. We don't even know what is in use in much-studied European languages. Tipped off by observing meaningful blinks in a Papuan language, we looked at blinks in Dutch and found that in that language long blinks (c. 400 ms) also carry systematic meaning (Hömke et al. 2018). That was certainly news to the multimodal community. There is every reason to think we simply haven't discovered most of the kinesic code. Perhaps to compute the number of such layers we can at least start from the degrees of freedom in each of the articulators. Animators and anatomists know the human hand has 27 degrees of freedom (DOFs) or movement potential; double that for both hands, add arm flexions (7 DOFs * 2), shoulder raises (2 DOFs * 2), torso twists (6 DOFs in the spine), head and neck (6 DOFs) – that's 98 degrees of movement. To that add Ekman's 44 Facial Action Coding System (FACS) or facial muscle movements, discernibly distinct directions of eye gaze, eye narrowing and so on. That is well over 150 potential signalling devices. Of course, they are not all in play at any one time, but that is the size of the orchestra that every speaker deftly manages, and abstention of movement can be significant too, as in the deadpan face. Every utterance is a complex multimedia performance – more like a Berlioz mass than the solo flute of linguistic descriptions!

Signals in the visual-motoric channel are by no means the only things we do not understand theoretically. The interactional uses of paralinguistic vocal parameters are also quite obscure. For example, Laver (1994: 199) outlines a complex system of phonation types, where the air passing through the larynx can have a turbulence heard as whispery, while low frequency air pulses yield a creaky voice or vocal fry, or the glottis is stretched to produce falsetto. In some languages these are used for phonemic contrasts, but in all languages they are available for signalling. In North America, creaky voice is typical of males speaking to females, but not to males (Wright et al. 2019): its low energy suggests confidence and relaxation. Similarly, there are many sub-phonemic vocalizations that can carry significance, the *mhm*s, clicks and sniffs that pepper interactions (Dingemanse 2020).

There is a more theoretical problem that needs addressing too. If we have a communication system with multiple channels and many layers, so that a speaker is emanating signals on say a dozen channels, how do we know what signals go together, that is how do we integrate all this (say a smile, a tease, a head shake and an eyebrow raise) into a single coherent message? The problem is exacerbated because the bits that demonstrably go together are not necessarily synchronous. For example, it has long been noted that gestures precede their 'lexical affiliates' by half a second or more – that is, one might gesture 'left' well in advance of saying 'left'. Similarly, a tease may be accompanied by a smile in the very last syllable, or a headshake long precede the mention of the thing negated. As a result we have what has been called a 'multimodal binding problem' as sketched in Figure 3 (Holler & Levinson 2019).

Although in interactive language use generally only one speaker speaks at a time (while simultaneously broadcasting on multiple layers non-verbally),

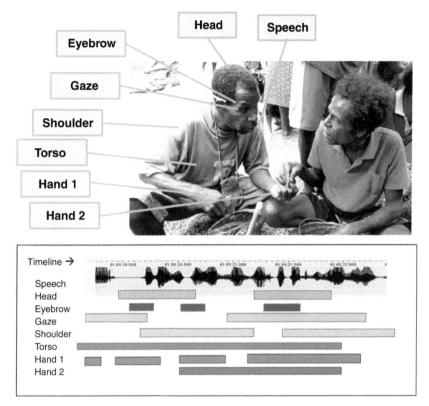

Figure 3 The multimodal binding problem: How do we know which signals on each of these tiers or layers belong together? How do we unite them into a coherent message? (*Photo S.C. Levinson*).

the recipient produces a running commentary of (mostly) non-verbal feedback, again on multiple layers. The recipient may lean forward open mouthed, then raise eyebrows, and smile as the other speaks. How and to what extent these responses play a feedback role in the incoming speech stream is currently almost entirely unexplored. We will return to this point later in the text.

Finally, we now have a rich set of ways of recording social interaction utilizing multiple cameras, head-mounted microphones, eye-gaze monitoring, breathing timing, pupil dilation, EEG-measurement and so on. A number of labs have built up impressive corpora with multiple measures, allowing new findings to emerge (see e.g. Kendrick et al. 2023). But at present we struggle to use these measures to full advantage, because our current understanding does not permit automatic coding of just the parameters relevant to participants; at the moment it must be largely done painstakingly by hand.

6 A Second Trick to Circumvent the Bottleneck: Dual Content, Word and Deed

6.1 The Known Knowns: Action Potential

Our engineer has quite a few further tricks up his sleeve in his efforts to get around the tight constraint on coding speed. A second trick is borrowed from a branch of cryptography called steganography. Steganography is the art and science of hiding one message within another. A classic example is the following (possibly apocryphal) message from a spy intercepted during the First World War:

(1)   Apparently neutral's protest is thoroughly discounted and ignored. Isman hard hit. Blockade issue affects pretext for embargo on by-products, ejecting suets and vegetable oils.

If one extracts every second letter in each word one obtains the intended message '*Pershing sails from NY June 1*'. The philosopher Grice repeats another (apocryphal) example: The British General Napier, when asked to chase some brigands in Northern India, ended up conquering the whole province of Sindh. He is said to have telegraphed the Latin phrase *peccavi* 'I have sinned' (he had disobeyed his orders), but the English translation is a pun for 'I have Sindh'. Here both the overt and the embedded message are relevant.

The principle is clear: you can double the content if you can send two messages simultaneously. Now, surprisingly perhaps, that is what we do the whole time. The philosopher JL Austin (1962) pointed out that when we utter an ordinary sentence in conversation we not only say things, we *do* things. Packaged up with the words is some kind of action. Austin called this an 'illocutionary act' carried by the 'locutionary act' of saying, and his key examples were things like promising, naming a ship, condemning a convict, or declaring war. In these cases, by an institutional arrangement, someone so empowered can create a new state of affairs just by following a precise procedure and uttering the appropriate words. He went on to point out that whenever we say something, we are in addition doing something, like making an undertaking that such-and-such is the case. By doing the one thing, we may (either by design or inadvertently) end up doing another: for example, if Vladimir casually remarks what a shame it would be if your daughter fell out of a window, you would be well advised to act cautiously. Such an indirect action (or actions, since they can be multiple) Austin called a perlocution (see Table 1).

The American philosopher Searle (1969) systematized Austin's observations, suggesting that such illocutionary acts or speech acts can be characterized by a set of conditions that they must meet in order to succeed. These felicity

Table 1 Dual and triple content in an utterance.

'Pretty daughter you have there, Yevgeny, shame if she fell out of a window'	
Locutionary acts	(Uttering the above sentences)
Illocutionary acts	Assessment; Expression of conditional regret
Perlocutionary act	Threat

conditions can then be used to suggest a universal set of possible speech act classes: representatives (assertions), directives (requests, questions), commissives (threats, promises), expressives (thankings, apologies …) and declarations (blessings, namings, condemnings and the like that rely on special institutional arrangements). Searle's systematization has been much used, but it has serious flaws – for one thing, it has lost the transactional quality whereby what is achieved by utterances depends on what the other makes of it (Austin called this 'uptake').

The idea that words *do* things as well as say things may seem metaphorical. But utterances really are actions that fit into action sequences. Consider for example standing at a supermarket checkout, where there's an exchange of verbal actions (announcing the total, thanking the customer) sequenced into a string of non-verbal actions (taking the money, handing back the change). Although the study of speech acts began in philosophy (the later ideas of Wittgenstein were critical here) and were systematized by Searle, it is conversational analysis (and the related interactional linguistics) that has thrown the most light on how an utterance comes to have the 'force' or action it actually has (see Levinson 2013a; Depperman & Haugh 2022). The interesting thing is that in general there is no one-to-one mapping between the form of words and the actions performed – the exceptions are just those things Austin initially focussed on, like being pronounced guilty or being declared married. Otherwise, there is often and perhaps mostly a many-to-many possible relation between utterance form and action performed. So, while 'Have you ever tried a heat pack?' might seem built for doing conditional suggesting, in another context the form may just be a question (cf. 'Have you ever tried hang gliding?', although even that might be a conditional offer to tell a story). Although there are favourite forms for some classes of action (e.g. the 'Could you …', 'Would you … ' forms of English requesting), the relationship between form and function is complex (Drew & Couper-Kuhlen 2014).

Conversation analysts have found that besides the actions we have colloquial names for (things like requests, promises, suggestions, proposals, greetings) there are many kinds of actions that have a subliminal existence: for example pre-closings (the exchange of '*Well*'s before closing a phone call), pre-tellings ('*Did I tell you what happened on Friday?*'), repair initiators ('*Huh?*'), sequence-closing thirds ('*Ok*'), etc. (Schegloff 2007). They have identified the kinds of context – mostly sequential contexts of successive actions – together with forms that may predispose the recipient to attribute specific actions to utterances. If some such characterization can be found, and it is usually a loose family resemblance, conversation analysts talk of a recurrent practice, and they continue to collect new practices. It was when Schegloff (1996) noticed a new practice that he speculated that our current knowledge was just the tip of an iceberg, and that there might be hundreds of undiagnosed actions in current employment, the rest being Dark Matter, an analogy I've purloined for the title of this Element.

Despite the complexities here, it is pretty clear that this is a good trick: we can greatly amplify the informative content of utterances through encoding actions. In principle, a single utterance can unleash a great chain of actions: 'Have you ever considered dieting?' is not likely to just be an idle question, but a pseudo-innocent suggestion, and therefore an insult into the bargain. Even a simple repair initiator like 'What?', may also be suggesting that the prior action is in inappropriate. Every utterance is potentially double or triple barrelled. However, it is equally clear that how this system works is rather obscure, which brings us quickly to consider the associated Dark Matter.

6.2 The Associated Dark Matter: Finding Actions

How actions are mapped onto words is one of the most important and most puzzling domains of pragmatics. Any analysis of verbal interaction depends on some kind of attribution of action to utterances. Our theoretical understanding is hampered in multiple ways.

First, there is unclarity over whether even within a cultural group there is a finite list of potential actions (see e.g. Enfield & Sidnell 2017). Perhaps the system is entirely flexible, allowing the ad hoc invention of actions, a bit along the lines Wittgenstein suggested in his theory of language games: we can invent a new game in which utterances may play new roles (Levinson 1979a). Second, there has been no systematic comparison of speech act types across a good sample of unrelated cultures. Anthropologists have reported cultures where, for example, there are no promises as we understand them (Rosaldo 1982; Duranti 2015), since the inner commitment or sincerity is not something the locals put store by. So we have no idea whether there is some kind of universal inventory of speech act types, and if so what it is. The sentence types interrogative, declarative and imperative are mostly discernible across languages, but these tend to have surprisingly wide functions. It is clear that there are culture-specific speech acts – the very institutional cases that Austin initially focussed on (marrying, christening, condemning and the like) are clear cases in point. But it is possible that a core set of functions is universal (Tomasello 2008 suggested requesting, informing and sharing), and are supplemented by rich sets of culture-specific actions within idiosyncratic 'language games'.[9]

But by far the largest of our puzzles is how participants actually ascribe actions to utterances. One element of the puzzle is that despite the many-to-many possible mappings from utterances to actions, we apparently get it right nearly all the time. There are only a handful of systematic misreadings of action content noticed in the literature, and I have found only a few in years of trolling through transcripts. Moreover, when engaged in conversation, the phenomenology is certainty of ascription, not a continuous wonder at what the other means. A second element of the puzzle is that action ascription is fast and apparently effortless. Brain imaging suggests that speech act recognition can occur very early during the processing of an incoming turn – even within the first syllable or two, which is extraordinary (Gisladottir et al. 2018). In general, the turn-taking system in conversation is going to force very fast decision making, and early response planning, but since one responds to the prior action, it is clear that everything hangs on fast action ascription.

A real mystery is how this mapping of function or action onto utterances is done so efficiently and fast. The many-to-many mapping and the possible open-endedness of the functions already appears to pose a formidable cognitive problem. Add to that the speed and accuracy and we have a serious scientific puzzle: How does it work? There are two main suggestions in the literature, but they both have their problems. One of them (championed by early AI research, Herb Clark and myself at various times)[10] imagines that to understand an utterance one reconstructs the likely communicative goal of the speaker. This would just be a special case of our general way of understanding other humans' actions: we interpret behaviour on the assumption that it is goal driven. Seeing someone approach a door and put their hand in a pocket, we jump to the conclusion they are fishing for a key to open the door. In the same way, when in receipt of an utterance one asks what is the speaker's purpose here? If a student asks outside the classroom 'Is this the lecture on pragmatics?', one might reply 'No, you want Room 208' foreseeing that they intend to go to the pragmatics lecture, so helping them on their way. Sometimes quite

---

[9] As explored in the ethnography of speaking (see Bauman & Sherzer 1989)
[10] Allen & Perrault 1980, Clark 1996.

opaque intentions can nevertheless be discerned by interlocutors. Consider the following phone call (from Levinson 1983: 343), where the initial question is taken by the recipient to be fishing for an offer – a presumption that turns out to be right.

(2)   C: Hullo I was just ringing up to ask
                  if you were going to Bertrand's party   ← *Q, Pre-Request*
                                                            – *Fishing for offer*
           R: Yes I thought you might be   ← *Joke at transparency*
           C: Heh
           R: Yes would you like a lift?   ← *Offer*
           C: Oh I'd love one

So one theory would be that we are continually in the business of goal reconstruction – building models of what drives the other agent's utterances and actions. This has the virtue of accounting for how a single turn at talk could perform multiple actions: a proximate goal can have an ultimate goal behind it. One problem for this theory is how far back do we go? In the phone call above, R guesses that C wants to know if R is going to the party as a precondition for asking for a ride; but does R also start speculating about why C wants to go the party, and if not, what stops the chain of inferencing? Goals are embedded in higher order goals recursively. A second problem is that we have no theory about how this can be done. Seeing someone buy some wine doesn't tell us what they want it for; perhaps he will drink it, perhaps it is a gift, perhaps he wants to stock it in case of visitors. A logic of practical reasoning will take you from desires to ends that will satisfy them, but not in reverse, from the ends to the desires. A third problem is all this looks like very intensive cognitive reasoning, but mapping actions onto utterances has to be very fast if the response is not to be delayed.

The alternative theory is simpler. We just build up a vast association network between utterance forms, contexts and actions. So saying 'Can you reach the butter?' will just by familiarity come to be taken to be a request. When conversational analysts talk about practices, perhaps this is what they have in mind. A central observation in CA is that sequential context in a series of actions is often a powerful heuristic. So checking a precondition for an action is likely to foreshadow that action, hence the quick inference that the caller in example (2) above was going to ask for a ride. But that question is at the very beginning of a telephone call, just like 'Can you reach the butter?' might come out of the blue. So initial actions, for example the first parts of adjacency pairs (sequences like questions–answers, requests–compliances, etc.), often do not have much contextual support. Interactional linguists would add that prosody and linguistic nuance might play a central role in identifying action, but still it does not seem at all plausible that utterances are always or even often action-determinate just by virtue of their form.

There are other problems with this theory too. We do know that giant association engines can do marvels, as shown by current AI natural language processors. But they do require vast training data. If we were behaviourist machines like this, associating conversational sequence, context and form with actions, we would expect children (given less exposure) to make lots of action-ascription errors, and I don't know any evidence for this. We would also expect the associations to have a probabilistic character, and then we ought not to be surprised if we misattribute actions. But that is not the phenomenology at all, as already remarked. Then there is the striking fact that novel or unusual form-function mappings do occur from time to time, and don't seem to cause much trouble. A couple of examples are as follows:

(3)   A: I could eat the whole of that cake ← *compliment*
        B: Thanks!   *(takes prior as compliment)*

(4)   A: I also have a dog
        B: Oh I'm sorry ← *disqualification for rental, after Sacks 1968)*

The business of action ascription is the beating heart of language use – the most vital part of pragmatics. Arguably, the whole point of language is just this, to deliver actions: assertions, questions, re-assurances, proposals, etc. The sequence of these is the thread that ties together conversational activity. And our failure to understand how it actually works should be rather humbling.

7 A Third Trick to Circumvent the Bottleneck: Choice of Message Form

7.1 The Known Knowns: Utterance-Type Meanings

Our engineer has another trick up his sleeve. If we have prearranged conventions, we can smuggle in some extra meaning. 'One if by land, two if by sea' was the signal that Paul Revere organized to be displayed in a Boston church tower to warn whether the British were coming by land or by sea. More elaborately, the BBC arranged to tell the French Resistance that the Normandy landings had begun by broadcasting verses of Verlaine's. This is an old trick: in the Old Testament, Jonathan arranges to tell David, who is hiding near the archery practice, whether it is safe to show himself according to whether he tells his boy to fetch the arrows from this side or the far side.

A more subtle mode of signalling is to arrange that the mere choice of words or the manner of speaking carry the intended signal.

There is a large range of tricks of this sort to amplify what we mean. They are all based on the choice of words or constructions or manner of production, which will, by tacit arrangement, signal specific messages. I will call these utterance-type inferences, since the choice of the general character of the formulation carries the extra meaning. The most celebrated of these are Grice's (1967/1989) conversational implicatures. The tacit arrangement in this case are Grice's maxims of cooperative conversation. My version of these maxims (Levinson 2000) boils down to three simple, largely iconic heuristics:

(1) What isn't said, isn't meant (roughly Grice's Quantity 1 maxim)
(2) Simple form suggests normal extension (close to Grice's Quantity 2 maxim)
(3) Abnormal form suggests abnormal extension (Grice's maxim of Manner).

Given the first of these rules of thumb, if I say 'I've eaten some of the cookies', I suggest conversationally (conversationally implicate is the technical term) that I have not eaten all of them, because if I had meant 'all' I should have said so. These are the well-known Horn scales, and they operate wherever there are scales of communicative strength. So in the Avianca Flight 502 disaster (mentioned in Section 1.0), the failure of the crew to say 'emergency' rather than the 'urgent' they did say, led air traffic control to think that it was not an emergency.

The second and third of these rules of thumb work like this: If I say 'She opened the door' you will assume that she did it in the normal way by turning the handle, pushing the door, etc. If in contrast I say 'She caused the door to open', or 'She managed to open the door', you will assume (by rule of thumb (3)) that she did it in some other, special and unusual way. I once coined the paradoxical aphorism 'the less you say the more you mean' to capture the interaction between maxim (2) that encourages rich stereotypes and maxim (3) that inhibits them (Levinson 1987). So any equivalent way of saying the same thing will not necessarily carry the same inferences. It seems that in all cases we work with a metalinguistic principle of contrast (Clark 1987). We ask ourselves: why did she say it this way, when instead she could have said it that other way – either by using a stronger item on a scale, or by using a simpler, more compact expression. Such a principle may be presumed to carry over to prosody.

A huge amount of research has been devoted to Grice's maxims, and there are rival theories – apart from my own (Levinson 2000), the most prominent are Horn's version (Horn 1989) and Sperber and Wilson's (1986) relevance theory. They all rely on some kind of metalinguistic vigilance, in order to detect that additional inference is required.

A rather different kind of utterance-type meaning is so-called presupposition. These are inferences that again arise from the choice of words but seem more attached by convention. For example, the verb *regret* seems to presuppose the factuality of the thing regretted. So 'Sue regrets yelling at Tom' implies she did do so, and so does the negation ('Sue doesn't regret yelling at Tom'). It turns out that there is a very long list of English words and constructions that trigger inferences of these sorts that are invariant under negation (see e.g. Levinson 1983: 181–184). Presuppositions allow us to use more compact forms: instead of saying 'Sue thought Tom was an idiot and he is one' one could say 'Sue realized Tom was an idiot' with the same implication. Similarly, if I say 'The Dean has stopped making sexist comments', I do not need to add that he used to do so – that is presupposed. Once again there are competing theories of presuppositions, some theorists holding that they are part of semantic content, others holding that they are so-called conventional implicatures – forms with specific usage conditions like honorifics for example – and others like Atlas (2005: Ch. 3) and myself thinking that they may not actually be so distinct from conversational implicatures of the Gricean sort. Relevant here though is that these inferences, like conversational implicatures, are 'defeasible', that is, they can be lifted or cancelled without contradiction either by a context they do not fit, or by explicitly querying them, as in 'The Dean has stopped making sexist comments, if indeed he ever did do so'. In this way they share with conversational implicatures their presumptive but cancellable quality. Regardless of which theory you buy, presuppositions are additional inferences that can be smuggled through the production bottleneck by a careful choice of linguistic expression or construction.

But the pay-off of having presuppositions is amplified by the fact that presuppositions can be used to trigger yet more inferences. So an utterance like 'He bought a new lawnmower, pulled the cord and the motor started' presupposes that there is a unique identifiable cord and similarly an identifiable motor, but it also strongly suggests that the cord and the motor are parts of the lawnmower, and pulling the cord started the lawnmower. These so-called 'bridging inferences' (Clark 1977) are things we read in to an utterance, not meanings inherent in the sentence. Although triggered by presuppositions, bridging inferences themselves can be attributed to a version of the second simple heuristic (2) mentioned earlier that licenses, from minimal specification, maximally informative or stereotypical interpretations.

These methods of amplifying coded content by virtue of prearranged rules of thumb or pre-packaging of default assumptions are some of the most productive ways of circumventing the coding bottleneck. They are also among the most researched topics in pragmatics. But that does not mean we fully understand them, in fact there are plenty of residual puzzles, to which we now turn.

7.2 The Corresponding Dark Matter: How Many Principles?

Most theories of implicature start off from Grice's maxims, and attempt to revise or improve them. (An exception may be relevance theory, although it also relies on a principle of relevance; Sperber & Wilson 1986.) Grice viewed these as a natural side product of rational cooperation. The idea, as pointed out in the preceding section, is that such tacit rules of use generate unsaid overlays on messages. Most empirical work has been devoted to generalized conversation implicatures – that is, ones that are generated by metalinguistic considerations of what else could have been said. These are mostly the scalar and manner implicatures. The contrast with what else might have been said provides a search heuristic for what is actually implicated (so 'He caused the car to stop' makes one ask why didn't the speaker say 'He stopped the car' – presumably because he didn't do it in the normal manner). Similarly, failure to answer directly a question like 'Is John in?', substituting, say, the response 'His coat is on the hook' will implicate the recipient does not know the answer for certain. But outside constrained contexts like these we have no real understanding of how implicatures are calculated. The whole of what Grice called 'particularized' implicatures (like the suggestion that John is not far away because his coat is on the hook) remain much more puzzling: How does a recipient find from the forest of possibilities just the implicatures intended within just a few hundred milliseconds? Relevance theory – one of the few theories brave enough to tackle particularized implicatures – talks gaily of adding assumptions as required to derive something of relevance. But AI approaches to this problem – which is essentially Peirce's problem of abduction (Douven 2021) – show that even in highly constrained domains finding an algorithm that will do anything like this is very problematic (Blokpoel et al. 2018). So here is a huge open question about how we process these inferences.

Grice went on after introducing his maxims to add 'There are, of course, all sorts of other maxims (aesthetic, social or moral in character), such as "Be polite" … and these may also generate nonconventional implicatures' (Grice 1989: 28). We might wish he had said more! Are there lots more maxims that we have failed to notice? The crucial test for such a maxim would be that both in its observation and in its violation it should generate specialized inferences.

I think there is plenty of room for suspicion that we are missing principles of language use which are hidden in plain view. Robin Lakoff (1973) and Geoffrey Leech (1983) have run with politeness maxims, following Grice's tip off, while Brown & Levinson (1978/1987) suggested instead that 'face motivations' might lead one to veer away from otherwise rational behaviour. One principle that has been suggested requires the acknowledgement of local opinion: 'When expressing an opinion on a topic that has been previously discussed, a speaker should correctly indicate the cultural standing of that view in the relevant opinion community' (Strauss 2004: 161), as in: 'If there are more Spanish people in the country than there are, you know, more Spanish-speaking people than Americans, then-*oh that was riddled with political incorrectness*' (op. cit. 178). It's not quite clear that such a maxim would generate inferences, beyond the inference that if one doesn't distance oneself from the consensus, one subscribes to it.

But I suspect that we are having a failure of the imagination here. So, let me fly a few kites, half-baked suggestions for further maxims.

(i) Acknowledge the presence of another

Clearly such a maxim is context-bound: it doesn't hold in big cities or crowded concourses. But in small enclosed spaces, for example an elevator, there does seem to be some such obligation, if only to exchange a smile, or more minimally to avoid invasion of each other's personal space. Following the maxim acknowledges the personhood of the other, while failure to do so may generate the inference that one is withholding that acknowledgement. Goffman in his doctoral thesis (1953) noted that non-acknowledgement of presence was precisely the behaviour around slaves in the pre-bellum Southern states of the USA. Such a maxim might be derived from politeness considerations, but it seems more basic than that.

(ii) Match the channel, medium and tone

It is a fact noted by sociolinguists and social psychologists that people tend to 'accommodate' to each other's dialect, accent or – in bilingual settings – language (Giles & Smith 1979), that is, they modulate their own speech patterns to more closely match the other's. Doing so indicates that for current purposes one is identifying as a co-member of some group or category (however large). Violating it – choosing a different language or dialect, or speaking much louder than the other – suggests dissimilation, putting social space between oneself and the other. In this way there seem to be inferences available both from following the maxim and flouting it, just as with Grice's core maxims.

(iii) Stay within the topic and/or activity, or signal otherwise

Unfortunately, topic structure is a subject clothed in relative obscurity (but see Yang 2019): there seem to be rules for opening new topics, transitioning to new ones, and closing topics down. But a turn at talk that doesn't announce a change of topic will be inspected for its connection to prior subject matter. So not marking an utterance as a departure implicates that it should be understood as 'about' the ongoing topic, while marking the utterance as a departure (e.g. with

'Oh, I forgot to say ...') may implicate haste or rudeness if it breaks the topic flow. Similar remarks may hold for activities: so, in a seminar, other things being equal, a turn at talk will be understood to be germane to the subject matter and appropriate to the activity. Teachers may strive to keep their students within the bounds of an activity, for example, by insisting on an intervention being phrased as a question.

These are light-hearted suggestions, but perhaps they will spur more serious investigations.

For any set of maxims or rules of proper interactional engagement, the question arises whether or not they are essentially culture-invariant. Grice's maxims, based on rational behaviour, might seem immune to cultural variation, but a number of authors have challenged this (e.g. Ochs Keenan 1976; Senft 2008; Ameka & Terkourafi 2019). Some of these challenges may miss the mark: the maxims are not rules of behaviour, they are default assumptions acting as inferential triggers. So if you very clearly fail to provide enough information to answer a question, you clearly signal that you can't or don't want to answer it. Nevertheless, if there genuinely are societies, where for example, no first maxim of Quantity ('make your contribution as informative as is required') obtains, then it follows there should be no Horn scales, and one may expect to find a monomorphemic lexicalized expression meaning 'nall' (not all), and so forth for all the predictions found in Horn 1989. Similarly, for the maxim of Manner ('be perspicuous'): If there is really no Manner maxim or the like in operation, then such a language should have no systematic meaning differences between compact phrases and periphrastic ones, for example between items paralleling 'to close the door" vs. 'cause the door to close'. All this needs investigation – but as far as I know, there are no such studies.

Finally, turning to presuppositions, this was a hot topic in the 1970s and 1980s, but since then has rather gone off the boil (but see Beaver et al. 2021). One of the most basic questions remains unresolved: Where do presuppositions come from? Some authors think they are arbitrary little nuggets of conventional meaning. Others (including myself) suspect they are derivable by general principles like Grice's maxims. A crucial datum here would be how 'detachable' they are: how easy is it to find another expression that seems to mean exactly the same thing but lacks the presupposition in question? If it is easy, then the presupposition is clearly coded conventionally. If presuppositions are conventional overlays – so encoded in lexical items directly – then there would be no expectation that they would translate across languages readily. But an early exercise of my own seems to show that they do translate item-for-item across some unrelated languages (Levinson & Annamalai 1992), subject to grammatical restrictions. It is surely remarkable that the question of source or origin of such fundamentally important elements of meaning remains unresolved. There are many other puzzles too, for example concerning the intricate rules for 'projection' of different classes of presupposition (see Beaver et al. 2021).

Grice had invented a third category, neither a conversational implicature nor a semantic entailment, which he called conventional implicatures. Grice's exhibit A was the adversative conjunction *but*, which seems to have the same semantic properties as *and* with something added, a notion of contrast. Karttunen & Peters (1979) went on to suggest that presupposition triggers belong to this category, but in that case they should not readily translate, and it should be easy to find an alternative way of saying the same thing that lacks the trigger, which is counter-factual, as already mentioned. That leaves the category of conventional implicatures under-inhabited. I have suggested (following Grice on *but*) that many little discourse particles like *anyway, however,* or *besides* and many items of social deixis like honorifics belong to this category (Levinson 1979b).[11] The suggestion is that conventional implicatures might be particularly associated with deixis, that is with the local parameters of the context of utterance. This is another category of meaning that needs much more investigation.

Both presuppositions and conventional implicatures touch on the question of the exact nature of 'what is said' and its relationship to semantic representations and the pragmatic inferences they give rise to. This is a subject that has had persistent attention (e.g. Atlas & Levinson 1981; Carston 2002; Recanati 2004; Atlas 2005; Jaszczolt 2023) but many puzzles remain. Pragmatic inferences can clearly 'intrude' on semantic interpretation (Levinson 2000: Chapter 3), yet there must be a determinate semantic input to pragmatic reasoning, or else our reasoning would be forever chasing its own tail. There are intricate issues here beyond this small book, but I think it's fair to say that the jury is still out, pondering the solution (see Korta & Perry 2020).

8 A Fourth Trick to Circumvent the Bottleneck: Non-literal Uses of Language

8.1 The Known Knowns: How Language Use Goes on Holiday and Does Figures of Eight

In 1917, Marcel Duchamp stuck a urinal on top of a plinth, signed it 'R. Mott, 1917' and exhibited it as a work of art. This caused a great deal of excitement – an uproar might be a better description. And that was exactly what he intended. The juxtaposition of a urinal on a plinth in an art gallery suggested a whole slew of possible conclusions, amongst them that the art world stinks, anything is art if

---

[11] Interjections have had some recent attention: for example Heine 2023, Liesenfeld & Dingemanse, 2022.

you sign it, a manufactured item like a urinal is actually quite artful if you can look at it in a detached way, let's piss on art, and a whole load more!

Our engineer will borrow this trick. It's not a precision instrument, it's more like a shotgun or a blunderbuss, issuing a wide and diffuse spray of suggestions. Or perhaps, more like throwing a pebble in a pond, and seeing where the ripples go. But this sort of chain of suggestions clearly offers a way of once again avoiding that dreadful production bottleneck – we can mean a great deal more than we say, even indefinitely more.

Manny Schegloff once suggested[12] that in ascribing actions to utterances, the first thing you have to decide is: Is this serious or non-serious? 'Non-serious' uses of speech include jokes, teases, ironies, rhetorical questions and the like where the recipient has to detect first that it is counterfeit currency, and second what its purpose is. Delayed detection makes a good joke. Churchill was a master of the back-handed compliment: 'Mr Atlee is a commendably modest man with much to be modest about' or 'We can always count on the Americans to do the right thing, after they have exhausted all the other possibilities'.

The fact that we have a genre of non-serious uses of language opens up the possibility of the 'just joking' defence. So, when Trump addressing a police academy said 'When you guys (the police) put someone in the paddy wagon, **please do NOT be too nice**', his press secretary had to deny he meant 'rough up the detainees'. According to Senft (2008), in Trobriand culture any remark can be recast as 'just joking' (in *biga sopa* genre), but as the Trump example illustrates, the defence works best when combined with a figure of speech (here a litotes or negative understatement).

Figures of speech were already classified and studied in ancient rhetoric, and it is hard to say anything very new about them. Grice of course took the position that his maxims are the trip lines, which if flouted generate figurative meanings, but how exactly was left unclear. One modern development has been to point out the ubiquity of figures of speech in ordinary ways of speaking and their relation to analogical thinking; indeed perhaps we just *think* in a folk psychology peopled by metaphors like time is space, life is a journey, argument is warfare, and so on (Lakoff & Johnson 1980). Another development has been to show that words are so often coerced into new construals by a juxtaposition of context that the effect is almost imperceptible (e.g. in 'He began the sculpture', *begin* expects an event complement, and the sculpture must now be understood as a process, not a thing; Pustejovsky 1995). Some recent relevance theory approaches end up treating metaphor in just this way, as coercion into

---

[12] Schegloff, E. A. (2008). Prolegomena to the analysis of action(s) in talk-in-interaction. Paper presented at the Max Planck Institute for Psycholinguistics, Nijmegen, The Netherlands.

a construal (and thus as an 'explicature' in that jargon; Carston 2002). Many modern approaches treat metaphors and the like as semantic/grammatical anomalies or categorical misfits (however mild) from which an inference about speaker meaning is derived by cognitive means guided by pragmatic assumptions (see Hills 2022 for review). Irony on the other hand relies on the mismatch between what is said and what is taken for granted, the disjunction invoking the contrast between the actual situation and the situation in which the ironic statement would be true (so Wilson & Sperber 2004 liken irony to a quotation where the speaker's attitude – outrage, amusement, ridicule or the like – must be inferred from the contrast between the actual and the described situations).

Our question here is how the tropes can be employed by our engineer to circumvent the production bottleneck, and the plan of course is to use the striking juxtaposition of ideas to trigger an avalanche of suggested notions. In this way, they can act like little haiku:

(5)   *This world?*
       Moonlit dew
       flicked from a crane's bill.
       (Eihei Dogen Kigen, loose translation/interpretation by Michael R. Burch).[13]

Most ordinary language is not so spectacular of course, but it is because of this triggering of potentially indefinite inferences that figurative language plays such an important role in cherished forms of literature or song.

8.2 The Corresponding Dark Matter: Finding the Message

Despite the two millennia of thought about figurative uses of language, there are plenty of residual puzzles. For most figures of speech, we have suggestions about how they are processed but no real algorithms, and that for a reason: given the cascade of inferences potentially triggered, the speaker's target inferences have to be narrowed down using many aspects of the conversational context, including the prior action sequence, the relationship between speaker and addressee, and such factors as the speaker's reputation and sense of humour. So, as for much in pragmatics, the actual mechanisms of understanding elude us.

A leading question is to what extent the tropes and figures of speech familiar from English and other European languages are particular to the Western tradition, and to what extent the same inventory of devices can be found across the languages of the world. On the view that metaphor, hyperbole and so on are just varieties of loose talk (Wilson & Sperber 2004), then we can expect to find

---

[13]　www.thehypertexts.com/Haiku%20Best%20Masters%20Translation%20.htm

them everywhere, although not necessarily enshrined and developed in a rhetorical or poetical tradition. On the view that cognition itself is indelibly metaphorical (Lakoff & Johnson 1980), we might even think that the very same metaphors would have cross-cultural currency – which seems certainly to be sometimes false (Kovecses 2005). Particular figures of speech may of course be constrained by grammatical resources (e.g. litotes of the kind 'I'll be not unhappy if he fails' depend on the availability of lexical negation). As for irony, although there are comparisons between well-known languages, I know of no large-scale comparison of ironic language use. In general, for all the figures of speech, it is unclear to what extent this is a literary phenomenon, that is, whether such uses of language are largely restricted to, or at least most elaborated in, languages with extensive literary traditions (which account for less than about 5 per cent of languages). But it is likely that all cultures make use of figurative language in bardic traditions, religious contexts or song styles – what is unclear is what use is made of the whole palette of possibilities and how pervasive that use is.

It has long been noted in the child language literature that metaphors cause comprehension difficulties in preschool children, although it remains a matter of debate how early children themselves use intended metaphors (Pouscoulous 2011; Falkum 2019). A late development might argue against the 'loose language' (relevance theory) account of metaphor, since loose language itself doesn't seem to be a problem for the child. The acquisition story is in this way pertinent to ongoing theory development. The acquisition of metaphorical abilities is clearly an active field of research, but again I do not think there is much systematic research in languages other than European ones, and certainly not in unwritten languages. If there are still plenty of residual questions for metaphor, the acquisition of other figures of speech (metonymy, rhetorical questions, understatement, irony, litotes and the like) belong more centrally in our Dark Matter – and again, one can expect findings here to reflect on central theoretical questions.

Potentially related to the acquisition story is the question of individual differences in the use and processing of figurative language. It is well known that people with pragmatic difficulties, including those on the autistic spectrum, have difficulty with figurative language use (but see Kasirer & Mashal 2014). Again, this might not be predicted by the 'loose language' hypothesis of relevance theory. This suggests that there is likely a part of the general population that also comprehends or uses figurative language with some difficulty. Findings of this sort would be of relevance for educational purposes, and we may hope that this becomes properly investigated.

A final topic that cries out for attention is the study of multimodal signals associated with spoken figurative language. Non-serious uses, like teases, are typically associated with a very late smile. Ironies are said to be accompanied quite often by eyeball rolling (Colston 2020), although this may be a side effect of dissent from the view literally expressed (see Clift 2021). Spatial metaphors are very likely associated with gestures, and more abstract metaphors may be too. But we know far too little about the extent to which in spoken interaction figurative language is 'flagged' in other non-verbal modalities.

9 A Fifth Trick to Circumvent the Bottleneck: Leveraging the Context

9.1 The Known Knowns: Trading on Common Ground

We come to the last trick we review here, namely the strategy of piggy-backing on the context.

One way of appreciating how important this trick is, is to think about how the proper usage of words requires the world to be a certain way. Consider the following nonsensical exchange from *Alice's Adventures in Wonderland* (Chapter VII) where the context doesn't meet the conditions that the language presumes:[14]

(6)   'Have some wine,' the March Hare said in an encouraging tone.
        Alice looked all round the table, but there was nothing on it but tea.
        'I don't see any wine,' she remarked.
        'There isn't any,' said the March Hare.

Or consider the utterance *'May we come in?'* (Fillmore 1971). The appropriate or felicitous use of this requires the context to conform to the following conditions: There must be an enclosure of some sort that includes the addressee but not the speaker, the speaker must have companions also outside, the addressee must have some authority to permit entrance that the speaker lacks, and the proposed motion is towards the addressee. In this sort of way utterances both conform to contexts and project them, allowing us to smuggle in our presumptions through the encoding bottleneck.

A first and obvious way we exploit the context is through deictic reference (as in *May we come in?*). We can avoid all sorts of descriptive complexities by simply pointing and saying 'this'. Philosophers do a big song and dance about deictic reference because it relativizes what is said to a particular speaker, recipient, time and place. It makes language a curious kind of coinage that

---

[14] www.gutenberg.org/cache/epub/11/pg11-images.html

changes its value according to context (puzzling toddlers in the process). But it saves vast coding complexities, and contributes enormously to utterance compactness – 'I am here' is such a saving over 'Steve Levinson is in the village of Bourn at 8:45 a.m. on July 28th 2023' (when I actually wrote this sentence). Deixis then rightly has a pride of place in every pragmatics textbook. The related process of anaphora again saves us repeating the descriptive identifiers of the protagonists in our stories.

The second most important way we exploit the context in order to condense our utterances is by presupposing whenever we can. I can say 'I'm sorry I'm late, the train broke down', and now you know without me separately stating it that I came by train. Observing how we actually use names in conversation, Sacks & Schegloff (1979) formulated the maxim 'oversuppose and undertell!'. The reason this can work is because there are ways to indicate tentative trial uses, for example by a questioning pitch or 'try marker'. So we can gently escalate as needed as in 'It turns out it was Ben? Ben Wallace? The man who lives in the apartment above me?'. The dangers of over-supposing can thus be mitigated by conditionally offering repair in advance. Presupposition, we have seen, in turn can trigger other inferences, so again presupposing rather than saying will greatly squeeze down what we actually have to say.[15]

A third important way in which the context can be used in the compression business is by the simple expedient of assuming that the recipient will add the current utterance as an additional premise to an existing stock of premises – the contents of background knowledge or prior discourse – and crank out any additional inferences. One of the attractions of relevance theory (or any incremental account of utterance content, for that matter) is the kind of account it gives of the following little interchange:

(7)   A: 'Fancy a coffee?'
         B: 'I need to sleep'

where the wish to sleep added to the fact that coffee is a stimulant, and stimulants interfere with sleep, allows us to crank out B's answer 'No!' Unifying the new utterance with the accumulated context offers an ever-enlarging set of premises for deriving inferences.

Interactive language use occurs not only in conversation but also in many institutional contexts. Again, any fixed arrangements can be exploited. I once made the mistake, towards the end of a lecture, of saying 'Next week, we'll look in detail at Austin's theory of illocutionary acts', only to find that I had thereby

---

[15] The term *presupposing* is here used in an everyday, interactional sense; the technical term *presupposition* refers to the ways in which such presumptions can be built into the structure of utterances (see Section 7.0).

unwittingly ended the lecture early as the students packed up their books and started to go! In the same way, we can start a committee meeting by saying 'Well, we seem to all be here'. Here, we can formulate a maxim of the sort: 'Mentioning the preconditions for starting an activity, or the preconditions for ending it, is a way of starting, or conversely ending, the activity in question'. This is possible because institutions are organized in rule-bound activities in which language plays a specific bounded role (these are Wittgenstein's language games). In these specific activities, particular but simple utterances can do very complex things. Consider 'Checkmate!', 'Guilty', 'Over', 'Order!' said respectively in a chess game, a court of law, a cricket pitch and the House of Commons (Levinson 1979a). Again, we leverage the context to condense what needs to be said to a minimum.

Conversational analysts have emphasized the importance of the conversational sequence, the ordered sequence of actions performed by a string of turns. In trying to grasp what action is being performed by an interlocutor, participants must follow the real estate adage 'location, location, location!'. Thus 'Okay' after a request has a different force than after 'How are you?' or after another 'Okay' where it presages leave-taking. Interestingly, conversationalists have to track the structure of such sequences sometimes far back, due to the potential for an elaborate embedding structure. The following example shows recursive embedding of adjacency pairs up to four or five levels deep (each level marked below) – deeper than any recursion in spoken language syntax incidentally (Levinson 2013a). Consider the following embedded structure in a service telephone call, where the depth of embedding is represented by levels labelled L1–L5:

(8)   Telephone call to an artists' supply store (abbreviated from Levinson 1983: 305)

> C: .. I ordered some paint, some vermillion. And I wanted to order some more, the name's Boyd (L1)
> R: Yes how many tubes would you like sir? (L2)
> C: ... What's the price now with VAT? (L3)
> R: I'll just work that out for you (L4)
> C: Thanks (L4)
> (10.0 second pause)
> R: Three pounds nineteen a tube sir (L3)
> C: Three nineteen is it= (L4)
> R: Yeah (L4)
> C: That's for the large tube? (L5)
> R: Well yeah it's the 37 ccs (L5)
> C: I'll just eh ring you back I have to work out how many I'll need (L2)

Conversational sequence provides a rolling context, which allows for massive condensations of content not only through anaphoric devices but also through ellipses. After initiatory actions – first parts of adjacency pairs like requests, offers and the like – responses are typically elliptical. Note in the following German example how the case marker in the response tracks the missing verb (accusative on the definite article): in some basic way the full sentence 'I would like to drink a white wine' has been computed then abbreviated to 'an(ACC) white wine'. That's the savings ellipsis buys you, so allowing us to slip sideways through the production bottleneck.

(9)   A: *Was möchten Sie trinken?*
        B: *Bitte einen Weißwein* (instead of *Ich möchte bitte einen Weißwein trinken*)

In this section we have reviewed perhaps the most important ways in which we can exploit the context to reduce our coding time. Deft leveraging of the context allows just the tip of the iceberg of communicated content to be exposed to the ears and eyes – the rest we can detect below the waves.

9.2 The Black Hole of Context

If there is a black hole in pragmatics it is the notion of context: the more you dig, the deeper you go – there doesn't seem to be an end to the factors that might be relevant to understanding a talk exchange (see Goodwin & Duranti 1992 for a selection of views). There's the setting in which we talk, the relationships between the interlocutors, their entire knowledge of their worlds, the current conversational sequence, the topic under discussion, all the previous conversations they have had, the superimposition and layering of activities (e.g. eating, drinking, priority talk organizing eating vs. other conversation) and the list goes on. There may not be a principled end to the list: as the prior section suggests, we leverage anything we can.

What is however Dark Matter worthy of investigation is the way in which each of these contributing factors is structured. It is that structure that gives affordances for exploitation for our compression purposes. For example, the deictic parameters recognized by a particular language allow abbreviated reference. Western philosophers assume an agent, a time, a location and (if they have thought about demonstratives) a gestural demonstration. But even for English we'll need more than that – certainly the addressee, spatial arrangements and the discourse context. In Kwak'wala subjects and objects have to be routinely marked for visibility to the speaker; other systems have exotic distinctions in elevation for demonstratives, or honorifics for person reference. In actual fact, the apparatus you need is quite complex, and varies for almost every language. There are some cross-cultural surveys of demonstratives in particular (charting the number of distinctions, Diessel 1999, or exploring usage in a limited number of languages, Da Milano 2007, Levinson et al. 2018). But there is much more to do in understanding cross-linguistic variation. Here is a domain crying out for the recording of multimodal behaviour across many languages. Until we have much more descriptive studies using video recording, serious generalization will evade us.

Another aspect of context that we know is highly structured is the sequential organization of conversation (Schegloff 2007). But again, we still know rather little about the universality or otherwise of these structures; the first cross-cultural comparison of a range of conversational structures covering a dozen languages is recent and suggests much may be invariant (Kendrick et al. 2020). Similarly, repair organization (specifically, how one signals comprehension problems) shows striking parallels across languages (Dingemanse et al. 2015). However, given the expected differences in the action inventories of different cultures, there is likely to be systematic variation in some notable respects. A related, relatively neglected domain is how syntactic structures are specialized for placement in these action sequences. This has been a focus of work in interactional linguistics (Couper-Kuhlen & Selting 2017), but a great deal more could be done here.

The study of many other aspects of context from this structural point of view seem quite neglected. Cross-cultural patterns in reference to persons and places have had some recent attention (Enfield & Stivers 2007; Mark et al. 2011) again revealing principles guiding the degree to which reference has to be descriptively explicit. Social relationships between interlocutors have of course a fundamental effect not only on what can be taken as given, but also on the interpretation of speech acts (Holtgraves 1994) and much else besides, in a way organized by local social structures. Many other aspects of context, like topical organization, remain fairly obscure.

But we come now to the central puzzle of context. We have to swim in a vast sea of attributed beliefs. In order to exploit background knowledge, we must assume mutual access to designated parts of it shared between us and our current interlocutors. But how do we judge what those parts are? There have been learned disputes about even the very form of these shared beliefs – do I believe that you believe that I believe ... (ad infinitum) that we see a table before us? Clark (1996: 96ff) offers a simpler resolution in the sharing of a basis for beliefs (e.g. the book in front of us can be presumed common ground because we share the basis for the belief, namely our co-presence with the book). But regardless of that, how do we make these fine judgements about what it is reasonable to presume? What dimensions of social organization make it likely that you and I share knowledge about some domain?

To appreciate the miracle of this consider that in order not to be the party bore I must not tell you anything you already know, and above all, not anything I have already told you. But this requires a vast inventory of whom I have told what to, boggling in its size and complexity. Consider too Sacks' (1967 (1995: 560ff)) observation that in the case of bad news, the order of the telling must be first to those most affected, a principle observed after every disaster. Again, this reflects a structured social organization, and it is this structure that apparently allows us to predict or recall what would and wouldn't be news to anyone. Without this ability to guess or recover shared background assumptions, our communications would either be redundant, or they would misfire on mistaken presuppositions. As mentioned, the principle of 'over-suppose' backed up with repair cuts us some slack, but that is all.

There is one other very powerful idea about how we handle context. Gumperz developed the concept of *contextualization cues* (see Levinson 2003 for concise exposition). The idea in a nutshell is that an utterance can carry with it, through modulation of lexicon, grammar and prosody, the very contextual frame within which it should be interpreted, a bit like a snail that carries its own house around with it. A simple example of this might be code-switching into a familial dialect or code to indicate a kinship context. This was Gumperz's answer to Minsky's 'frame problem', the computational problem of finding the right axioms to get the inferences that need updating. It is a powerful idea too little developed, which may help us to understand how we find our way in the black hole of context.[16]

9.3 Summarizing the Tricks for Circumventing the Production Bottleneck

Just to rapidly take stock of where we are, we've reviewed five tricks for escaping what seems like an absolute limit on the speed and efficiency of human communication, namely the production bottleneck. These tricks exploit the residual cognitive capacity to understand much more than what is actually said. The first trick was to multiply channels and modalities, and the main elements of Dark Matter were the neglected channels and layers and the 'binding problem' that unified multifarious signals into a coherent message. The second trick was to multiply the content by adding an action content to each utterance, adding illocution to locution. Here the Dark Matter is how we

---

[16] Incidentally, conversational analysts have long had a stricture, when analysing recorded conversations, to not import additional information about the context. Their argument has been that participants use what is in the here and now, and that at least is all that the analyst should use.

actually do action attribution, this key capacity on which human linguistic interaction rests. The third trick was to have a tacit agreement about how the form of an utterance might be taken to favour particular construals, using generalized conversational implicatures, presuppositions and the further bridging inferences they afford. Here many questions arise about the exact nature of that tacit agreement, and whether there may be many such maxims we simply have failed to spot. In addition, there is the continuing puzzle about where presuppositions come from – are they arbitrary conventions or systematic side-products? The fourth trick was the use of figurative or non-literal language that delivers a diffuse spray of possible inference chains – which do we follow and why? How cognitively complex is it to understand these forms of language use? The fifth trick was to exploit the context to maximal effect, by not saying what can be only minimally specified or presupposed. Here our central puzzle was how we know what others do and do not know, and the puzzle of how we keep track of what we've told and not told particular others. For each of our tricks there are major domains that we can see need studying but remain relatively unexplored. And across all domains there is a striking lack of information on the small, indigenous languages that form 95 per cent of language diversity in the world. Table 2 puts this in tabular form, just noting the main outlines of the argument. We turn now to an even bigger puzzle.

Table 2 Summary of the main points so far.

Tricks	Corresponding Dark Matter
1. Multimodality	1. Neglected modalities; The 'Binding Problem'
2. Dual or triple content: force and action	2. Action attribution
3. Utterance-type meaning: Generalized conversational implicatures, Presupposition triggers, Bridging inferences	3. Other possible maxims; Sources of Presuppositions
4. Tropes and Non-serious language	4. Coordination of understanding
5. Leveraging the context: -Entailments with background -Activity types -Conversational sequences	5. Structured Context; How we know what others know
	And the question of the cross-cultural applicability of all of the tricks

10 From Dark Matter to Dark Energy: A Central Mystery in Human Communication

We borrowed the concept of Dark Matter from our astrophysical brethren because it captures so nicely the sense of things indirectly ascertained, known to exist but whose nature remains unknown. There's enough pragmatic Dark Matter to keep many cohorts of PhD students busy, and as they push the boundaries they will find more.

But there's another astrophysical concept we can borrow: Dark Energy. The universe is expanding at an ever-accelerating rate, a finding from the study of supernovae that is contrary to all prior expectations where the predictions were that the expansion would slow down. The unknown invisible force that must be pushing all the constellations apart – at the very same time that Dark Matter tries to anchor them – has been dubbed Dark Energy. NASA now estimates Dark Energy makes up 68 per cent of the universe, Dark Matter 27 per cent and directly detectable bodies just 5 per cent or less.[17]

I want to borrow the idea of a pragmatic Dark Energy for whatever it is that propels our pragmatic system at the incredible speed it seems to operate at. Just like Dark Energy confounds our expectations of normal processes, so there is some kind of unknown energy that allows our pragmatic inference engines to run at speeds that confound psycholinguistic expectations.

To see this let's return to the details of our production bottleneck. Earlier, we gauged the pressure of the bottleneck by showing that the maximum bit rate for human speech is under 100 bits per second, and normal practice close to half that. But now let's turn the measure into speed, measured in milliseconds. Thanks to the meticulous work of Levelt and colleagues (Levelt 1989; Indefrey & Levelt 2004) we know with great precision the time course of mental and neural events involved in seeing a picture and saying its name. Suffice here to say that from the moment one has the concept to the moment anything comes out of your mouth takes at least 600 ms. If the concept is not primed and is out of the blue, or the word is uncommon, it will take nearer to 1000 ms (Bates et al. 2003). Over half of this time is involved simply in finding the phonological form and programming its articulation. It is not something therefore than can easily be expedited. Coding up a single simple clause from scratch takes about 1500 ms of cogitation in experimental settings (Griffin & Bock 2000).

Now recollect at the outset of this book that we said we are focussing on the interactive spoken use of language. The canonical form of spoken interaction is in the context of conversation, where participants take turns at talking.

---

[17] https://science.nasa.gov/astrophysics/focus-areas/what-is-dark-energy.

A substantial body of recent work has shown that turn-taking has remarkably stable temporal properties, both across persons and across languages and cultures (Stivers et al. 2009). Generally speaking, turns are short (around 2 seconds long on average), and they occur rapidly after one another, with only about 5 per cent of the speech stream in overlap (Levinson & Torreira 2015; Levinson 2016). Most surprisingly, dependent a bit upon the sample, the gap between turns is mostly only about 200–250 ms long. Now, 200 ms is the minimal human response time, the sort of time it takes an athlete to leave the blocks after the starting gun. A further psychological fact is that the more choices of response that are required, the more time it takes: choosing to press a red button given a high tone and a green one given a low tone will take around 350 ms, and the time increases with each added choice. To produce a coherent turn at talk involves of course a lot of choices, in terms of content, words and structure.

Now let us take that minimum 600 ms latency in speech production, what it takes to go from concept to beginning articulation, and plug this number back into the picture of rapid turn-taking with only 200 ms gaps. It is clear if Bob is going to respond in good time to Anne, he has to start planning his response well before Anne has finished speaking. The consequence is Bob has to do two things at once: listen to the end of Anne's turn and plan his own response, a kind of double tasking that should be very hard, especially because both tasks – production and comprehension – are using parts of the very same language machinery. Figure 4 makes the point diagrammatically. As soon as Bob grasps Anne's speech act (marked (1) in the diagram), he can begin planning his response, launching it (marked (2)) as soon as he detects that Anne's turn is ending – since 200 ms is the minimal human response time, one can expect an average 200 ms gap.

If this picture is right, then it has surprising consequences for pragmatics. First, before Bob can begin his planned response he must have decided what action or speech act Anne is producing, even well before she has finished – it is the action, after all, to which any response is directed. In effect Bob is going to have to predict what Anne was going to say about midway through her turn (turns are on average under 2 secs long, Bob's plan to respond with a sentence will take at least 1 second)! And well before she finishes Bob has got to have computed all those pragmatic inferences, explicatures, implicatures, presuppositions, bridging inferences and so forth, otherwise his response may be off-target.

But is the picture right? Psycholinguists are sceptical because they are reluctant to think we can do this kind of double tasking efficiently, or even perhaps the kind of prediction required. One can point to the fact that we often use little particles (*um, well, uh,* etc.) to buffer the start of our utterances

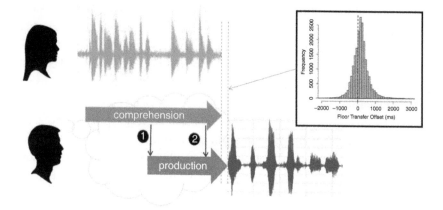

① Speech act recognition/prediction → production starts

② Prediction of upcoming turn completion → launch!

Figure 4 Overlap between comprehension and production:
The next speaker must begin planning his or her response midway while listening to the incoming turn. Inset is a typical distribution of responses times around 0, the end of the prior speaker's turn, implying planning for speaking must start well before 0 *(after Levinson 2016 with permission of the publisher)*

(Rühlemann 2020). But planning even one of those takes time. How long? Well, Rühlemann lists 15 common such interjections or particles. Now recollect that reaction time increases according to the number of alternatives that have to be selected from (think of yourself in the supermarket in front of all the soap powders): choosing between half a dozen possible response particles will take you over half a second, according to Hick's (1952) Law. So it is not clear that producing one of these particles will buy you so much time, as opposed to distracting you from getting on with the main job. Another observation is that sometimes conversation is more like a fugue, with each participant continuing their own part rather than responding to each other (Corps et al. 2022). That may be true, but if that was the norm, the kind of tight sequential organization detailed by Schegloff (2007) could hardly exist. Moreover, there is a whole body of corpus results and experimentation (reviewed in Meyer 2023) that tends to support the picture advanced by Levinson & Torreira 2015: an early detection of the incoming speech act, allowing early planning of response and then a late detection of the upcoming end of the turn which acts as the 'go' signal for the planned response (again see Figure 4).

I think the conclusion is inescapable that we are making all those complex pragmatic inferences incredibly fast, and for the most part accurately. The question then is: What is the Dark Energy that drives this system? We can only speculate.

I offer here just two suggestions. First, as we noted, face to face conversation is multimodal, and all the channels and layers are in action during the speaker's turn. But although recipiency – being an appropriate addressee – requires abstention from the main channel allowing the alternation of turns at talking, it by no means inhibits the other channels and layers. So-called backchannels, minimal verbal particles (*mhm, mm-hmm*, and the like) richly pepper transcripts of conversation (Liesenfeld & Dingemanse 2022), but there are also a myriad of multimodal signals indicating how an incoming turn is being received, with interest, surprise, dismay, etc. Gaze, facial expression, head nods, the shoulders and so on are involved in a dance that follows the timing of the other's words. Figure 5 provides a pictorial reminder of the complexity of all this, while suggesting the possibility that these micro-signals provoke slight online alterations of the speaker's own multimodal performance.

The interaction of speaker and addressee during the production of a single turn has perhaps been best studied in Japanese, where backchannels or *aizuchi* have a recognized status and seem to often accompany every increment of a turn as it is being produced. As Hayashi (2005) puts it,

> while turns-at-talk are often treated as if they were a bounded slot for speaking given to one participant at a time, they may be more adequately conceptualized as a temporally unfolding, interactively sustained domain of

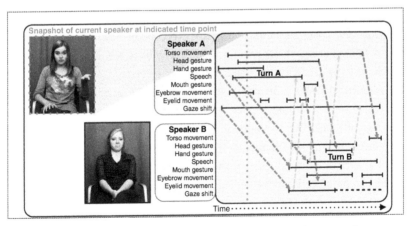

Figure 5 Cross-signalling between speaker and addressee using multimodal channels: Dotted lines show hypothetical causal links between signals across two speakers *(after Holler & Levinson 2019 with permission of the publisher)*

multimodal conduct through which both the speaker and recipients build in concert with one another relevant actions that contribute to the further progression of the activity in progress.

Multimodal exchanges in Japanese suggest that Western scholars, through privileging the verbal channel, may have failed to appreciate the degree to which the course of a turn is under moment by moment joint control.

In contrast to this picture Western psycholinguists have tended to argue that language production is 'ballistic': given the complexities of grammatical and phonological encoding, once language production has begun, it can be aborted and repaired, but otherwise cannot easily be modified on the fly. So an utterance is like an unguided missile with only a self-destruct button. But in contrast the conversational analysts have argued that turns can be seamlessly modified online, in order for example for an utterance to be retooled for a new addressee when the original one turns away (Goodwin 1981). These observations suggest indeed that utterances can be modified online in response to addressee feedback. If so, then mutual understanding is potentially being negotiated syllable by syllable, as it were, and this may help to account for the amazing speed at which we can respond.

Another suggestion about the nature of the Dark Energy of verbal interaction is related. Exploring embedded sequences, where one adjacency pair is embedded within another, I found (as mentioned earlier) much deeper embedding in interactive structure than can be found in grammar (Levinson 2013a). Now, syntax has been held up by Chomsky as the prime locus of recursion, and thus perhaps as the fount of all our higher order cognitive abilities. Psychologists have suggested that our failure to produce or understand centre-embeddings beyond two or three deep is due to the limits of our mental short-term memory (Gibson 1998). But these limits are gaily exceeded by adjacency pairs embedded within adjacency pairs (see Section 8), which are the joint product of two minds. Is there then a way in which interaction, by engaging two minds at once, somehow doubles our individual cognitive capacity? Consider how outsourcing our cognition to for example an electronic calculator helps us think; and how we can also outsource our cognition to other people, as in a quiz game for teams (Levinson 2023). If in interaction we are partly outsourcing our computing to another person, that might give us an inkling of the nature of the Dark Energy of human communication. Meanwhile, the mystery remains.

11 Some Further Targets for Future Research

There are many targets for future research beyond those we have touched on by exploring the edges of the known pragmatic world. Let me list here a few of the more obvious outstanding global questions.

1. How are utterances modulated to express all the fine grain of significant social relationships? Much has been written about politeness, but less about how we express like vs. dislike, support vs. disdain, empathy vs. coldness, trust vs. distrust, enthusiasm vs. boredom, honesty vs. dishonesty, faithfulness vs. unreliability, devotion vs. non-commitment and so forth. But these qualities are what cement, or alternatively dissolve, the social relationships that build our societies.

2. There are individual differences in pragmatic understanding, as in any other human performance. At the one end we have the pragmatic deficits, autism spectrum, attention deficit hyperactivity disorder (ADHD); specific language impairment (SLI), social pragmatic communication disorder (SPCD), all categories in the standard medical handbook, *Diagnostic and Statistical Manual of Mental Disorders* (DSM). Diagnosis relies heavily on interactive peculiarities. But what in precise, measurable pragmatic terms signals out the communication styles of each of these syndromes? There is some engagement between pragmatics and autism research, but pragmatics could offer much clearer baselines and norms for normal behaviour and its variability. We pragmaticists have the precise tools for studying deviancy in for example turn-taking timing, gaze behaviour, gesture, topical coherency, repair initiation, backchannel usage and the like.

3. At the other end of human variation, we have hyper-skilled language users. These are people with remarkable interactional grace, or rhetorical prowess, or 'the gift of the gab'. It is from this group that we draw most of our entertainers, newsreaders and politicians. What does their gift actually consist in? It is easy to forget that until quite recently most of the societies in the world had fluid political systems where rhetorical prowess was the critical ingredient in leadership. But what exactly this prowess consists in is rather unclear. What makes the current batch of populist leaders such apparently successful communicators?

4. Although it seems probable that there is a universal base for human communicative interaction (my 'interaction engine', Levinson 2019), there are clearly many culture- and language-dependent practices. What then happens in the minds of multilingual speakers? Do they operate with one generalized set of inferential practices, or switch between systems when they switch between languages?

5. Developmental pragmatics had a good head start in the 1970s and specific topics like joint attention, early deictic uses, early turn-taking, later implicature understanding or narrative construction have had some good attention (Hickmann 2008). But I think there is a great deal we do not know, for example the developmental trajectory of complex sequential structures or action ascription, the acquisition of the full range of multimodal resources and so on.

6. The pragmatics of sign languages lags behind the study of sign grammar and lexicon. There are reasons for this – even distinguishing gesture from sign can be hard in the sign channel. Still we can ask: do we find the same range of implicatures (e.g. Horn scales) in sign, are the mechanisms of action ascription comparable to spoken languages, how fully does sign exploit the multiple articulators to get around the coding bottleneck, what is the measured bit rate for sign communication and what channels and layers carry the most information?

7. How can pragmatic expertise be used to improve human–machine interaction? Should one train the human end or the machine end? Is it actually possible or safe to make a machine without a mind interact usefully and reliably with, for example, people with disabilities?

8. Can we apply insights from human pragmatics to the pragmatics of animal communication? Do other animals also wrestle with a coding bottleneck, so that they also rely on inferential communication?

9. A related question is whether there is a general pragmatic theory that holds for any communication system on the planet. Consider that there are many striking parallels between human language and DNA. Languages have on average about thirty phonemes, DNA has four letters or nucleotide bases; languages combine their phonemes into some hundreds of syllables, while DNA triplets of bases code for twenty amino acids; languages use their syllables to construct c. 20,000–30,000 words in productive use, while DNA uses its amino acids to construct c. 20,000 human proteins. Now, human language has a pragmatics that can delete, change and augment the meaning of the words. DNA is an instructional code, but arguably language also exists to deliver actions. DNA has its own pragmatics called epigenetics – an extra layer of information that can delete, change and augment the production of proteins. Like language pragmatics, epigenetics aids in adapting the 'message' to the context and the environment. Do some of the same 'tricks' hold in genetics that hold in languages? This is surely a very interesting question. The comparison is interesting too from a bit rate or speed of encoding perspective. It takes as we have seen something over 600 ms to produce a word; it takes something over 20 seconds for DNA via RNA and mRNA to assemble a protein.[18] Perhaps that makes us appreciate that even though our language encoding rate is a bottleneck, it is in comparative perspective remarkable. The

---

[18] There may also be an interesting multimodal analogy too, Tanya Freedman points out to me. Multiple ribosomes can simultaneously synthesize proteins, and alternative splicing of mRNA can produce multiple different forms of protein from a single gene. Epigenetic processes can also serve to limit the search space for appropriate gene expression, much like pragmatic processes resolve language–action mappings.

wonder increases when one appreciates that DNA has been evolving for four billion years, while spoken language has probably been around for at most one million. But the question we're asking is: Is there a general theory of pragmatics that applies to all the coding systems in our world?

12 Coda

The human elite capacity is communication. Other animals can fly as high as a jet plane or swim faster than a battleship,[19] but we have this unique ability to communicate thoughts of arbitrary complexity. This extraordinary ability rests on a pragmatic base. That base I have called 'the interaction engine' (Levinson 2019); it's an instinct to communicate through interaction. It is this inferential ability that underlies the learning of languages by children. The development of this ability has clearly played a crucial role in human evolution, spurring language origins. The role of pragmatics has been not merely to fill the available gap between the encoding bottleneck and our comprehension capacities, it is also the machine tool that makes and remakes the coding system in the first place during language acquisition.

The body of observations that we have built up in pragmatics about this exceptional ability makes us custodians of fundamental knowledge about the roots of human communication, and thus about the wellsprings of human social interaction, social relationships and culture. Many other disciplines are in need of input from the specialities we control: All the branches of the language sciences of course, but also all the sciences of society and social relationships, the medical sciences that deal with abnormal human behaviour or capacities, behavioural genetics and the study of animal behaviour. We have a duty to use the knowledge we have acquired in places where it is clearly required, for example in producing norms for diagnostic purposes, or advising in the construction of artificial agents.

Although over the last half century we have acquired a great deal of useful knowledge and built up a body of theory that directs our work, we remain too conservative in theory, method and topics embraced. I hope this little book will encourage younger scholars to go for the unexplored stars in a spirit of adventure.

---

[19] For the sceptical, Rüppell's vulture can fly at 37,000 feet (11,000 m), while the Indo-Pacific sailfish can swim at 68 mph (110 kph)!

References

Abercrombie, D. 1968. Paralanguage. *British Journal of Disorders of Communication*, 3, 55–9.

Allen, J. F. & Perrault, C. R. 1980. Analysing intention in utterances. *Artificial Intelligence*, 15, 143–178.

Ameka, F. K. & Terkourafi, M. 2019. What if … ? Imagining non-Western perspectives on pragmatic theory and practice. *Journal of Pragmatics*, 145,72–82 S0378216619300268. https://doi.org/10.1016/j.pragma.2019.04.001.

Atlas, J. D. 2005. *Logic, Meaning and Conversation*. Oxford: Oxford University Press.

Atlas, J. D. & Levinson, S. C. 1981. It-clefts, informativeness and logical form: Radical pragmatics (revised standard version). In P. Cole (ed.), *Radical Pragmatics*, New York: Academic Press, pp. 1–62.

Austin, J. L. 1962. *How to Do Things with Words*. Oxford: Clarendon.

Bates, E., D'Amico, S., Jacobsen, T. et al. 2003. Timed picture naming in seven languages. *Psychonomic Bulletin & Review*, 10, 344–380. https://doi.org/10.3758/BF03196494.

Bauman, R. & Sherzer, J. (eds.). 1989. *Explorations in the Ethnography of Speaking* (2nd ed., Studies in the Social and Cultural Foundations of Language). Cambridge: Cambridge University Press.

Beaver, D., Geurts, B. & Denlinger, K. 2021. Presupposition. In E. N. Zalta (ed.), *The Stanford Encyclopedia of Philosophy* (Spring 2021 Edition), https://plato.stanford.edu/archives/spr2021/entries/presupposition/.

Blokpoel, M., Wareham, T., Haselager, P., Toni, I. & van Rooij, I. 2018. Deep analogical inference as the origin of hypotheses. *The Journal of Problem Solving*, 11(1), Article 3. https://doi.org/10.7771/1932-6246.1197.

Brown, P. & Levinson, S. C. 1987. *Politeness: Some Universals in Language Usage*. Cambridge: Cambridge University Press. (First published 1978 in *Questions and politeness*, E. Goody, ed., Cambridge University Press).

Carnap, R. & Bar-Hillel, Y. 1952. *An Outline of a Theory of Semantic Information, Technical Report 247*. Cambridge, MA: Research Laboratory of Electronics, Massachusetts Institute of Technology. https://dspace.mit.edu/handle/1721.1/4821.

Carston, R. 2002. *Thoughts and Utterances: The Pragmatics of Explicit Communication*. Oxford: Blackwell. ISBN 978–0631214885.

Clark, E. V. 1987. The principle of contrast: A constraint on language acquisition. In B. MacWhinney (ed.), *Mechanisms of Language Aquisition*, Hillsdale, NJ: Lawrence Erlbaum Associates, pp. 1–33.

Clark, H. 1977. Bridging. In P. N. Johnson-Laird & P. C. Wason (eds.), *Thinking: Readings in Cognitive Science*, Cambridge: Cambridge University Press, pp. 411–20.

Clark, H. 1996. *Using Language*. Cambridge: Cambridge University Press.

Clift, R. 2016. *Conversation Analysis*. Cambridge: Cambridge University Press.

Clift, R. 2021. Embodiment in Dissent: The eye-roll as an interactional practice. *Research on Language and Social Interaction*, 54(3), 261–76. https://doi.org/ 10.1080/08351813.2021.1936858.

Colston, H. 2020. Eye-rolling, irony and embodiment. In A. Athanasiadou & H. Colston (eds.), *The Diversity of Irony*, Berlin: De Gruyter Mouton, pp. 211–35. https://doi.org/10.1515/9783110652246-010.

Corps, R. E., Knudsen, B. & Meyer, A. S. 2022. Overrated gaps: Inter-speaker gaps provide limited information about the timing of turns in conversation. *Cognition*, 223, 105037. https://doi.org/10.1016/j.cognition.2022.105037.

Coupé, C., Oh, Y., Dediu, D. & Pellegrino, F. 2019. Different languages, similar encoding efficiency: Comparable information rates across the human communicative niche. *Science Advances*, 5, eaaw2594. https://doi.org/10.1126/ sciadv.aaw2594.

Couper-Kuhlen, E. & Selting, M. 2017. *Interactional Linguistics: Studying Language in Social Interaction*. Cambridge: Cambridge University Press. https://doi.org/10.1017/9781139507318.

Darwin, C. [1872]1998. *The Expression of the Emotions in Man and Animals*. Oxford: Oxford University Press. (Originally, London: John Murray).

Da Milano, F. 2007. Demonstratives in the languages of Europe. In P. Ramat & E. Roma (eds.), *Europe and the Mediterranean as Linguistic Areas: Convergencies from a Historical and Typological Perspective*. Amsterdam: John Benjamins, pp. 25–47.

Depperman, A. & Haugh, M. 2022. *Action Ascription in Interaction*. Cambridge: Cambridge University Press.

Diessel, H. 1999. *Demonstratives. Form, Function, and Grammaticalization*. Amsterdam: John Benjamins.

Dingemanse, M. 2020. Between sound and speech: Liminal signs in interaction. *Research on Language and Social Interaction*, 53(1), 188–96. https://doi.org/ 10.1080/08351813.2020.1712967.

Dingemanse, M., Roberts, S. G., Baranova, J. et al. 2015. Universal principles in the repair of communication problems. *PLOS ONE*, 10(9), e0136100.

Douven, I. 2021. Abduction. In E. N. Zalta (ed.), *The Stanford Encyclopedia of Philosophy* (Summer 2021 Edition), https://plato.stanford.edu/archives/sum2021/entries/abduction/.

Drew, P. & Couper-Kuhlen, E. 2014. *Requesting in Social Interaction.* Amsterdam: John Benjamins.

Duranti, A. 2015. *The Anthropology of Intentions.* Cambridge: Cambridge University Press.

Ekman, P., Ellsworth, P. & Friesen, W. 1972. *Emotion in the Human Face.* Oxford: Pergamon.

Enfield, N. & Stivers, T. (eds.) 2007. *Person Reference in Interaction: Linguistic, Cultural, and Social Perspectives.* Cambridge: Cambridge University Press.

Enfield, N. J. & Sidnell, J. 2017. On the concept of action in the study of interaction. *Discourse Studies,* 19(5), 515–35. https://doi.org/10.1177/1461445617730235.

Falkum, I. 2019. Metaphor and metonymy in acquisition: A relevance-theoretic perspective. In K. Scott, B. Clark & R. Carston (eds.), *Relevance, Pragmatics and Interpretation,* Cambridge: Cambridge University Press, pp. 205–17. https://doi.org/10.1017/9781108290593.018.

Fillmore, C. 1971. *Santa Cruz Lectures on Deixis.* Mimeo, Bloomington, IN: Indiana U. Linguistics Club (Republished 2015 as *Lectures on Deixis,* Stanford: CSLI.)

Floridi, L. 2010. *Information: A Very Short Introduction.* Oxford: Oxford University Press.

Frankfurt, H. 2005. *On Bullshit.* Princeton: Princeton University Press.

Gibson, E. 1998. Linguistic complexity: Locality of syntactic dependencies. *Cognition,* 68, 1–76.

Giles, H. & Smith, P. 1979. Accommodation theory: Optimal levels of convergence. In H. Giles & R. St. Clair (eds.), *Language and Social Psychology.* Baltimore: Basil Blackwell, pp. 45–65.

Gisladottir, R. S., Bögels, S. & Levinson, S. C. 2018. Oscillatory brain responses reflect anticipation during comprehension of speech acts in spoken dialogue. *Frontiers in Human Neuroscience,* 12, 34. https://doi.org/10.3389/fnhum.2018.00034.

Goffman, E. 1953. *Communication Conduct in an Island Community.* Unpublished PhD, University of Chicago, http://cdclv.unlv.edu/ega/documents/eg_phd.pdf.

Goodwin, C. 1981. *Conversational Organization.* New York: Academic.

Goodwin, C. & Duranti, A. 1992. *Rethinking Context.* Cambridge: Cambridge University Press.

Gransier, R., Peeters, S. & Wouters, J. 2023. The importance of temporal-fine structure to perceive time-compressed speech with and without the restoration of the syllabic rhythm. *Sci Rep* **13**, 2874. https://doi.org/10.1038/s41598-023-29755-x

Grice, H. P. 1957. Meaning. *Philosophical Review*, 66(3), 377–388.

Grice, H. P. 1967. *Logic and Conversation*. Mimeo, unpublished MS of William James Lectures, Harvard. Published in revised form in Grice 1989.

Grice, H. P. 1989 *Studies in the Way of Words*. Cambridge, MA: Harvard.

Griffin, Z. & Bock, K. 2000. What the eyes say about speaking. *Psychological Science*, 11(4), 274–9. https://doi.org/10.1111/1467-9280.00255.

Grosjean, F. 1979. A study of timing in a manual and a spoken language: American sign language and English. *Journal of Psycholinguistic Research*, 8(4), 379–405.

Hanks, W., Ide, S., Katagiri, Y. et al. 2019. Communicative interaction in terms of *ba* theory: Towards an innovative approach to language practice. *Journal of Pragmatics*, 145, 63–71.

Hayashi, M. 2005. Joint turn construction through language and the body: Notes on embodiment in coordinated participation in situated activities. *Semiotica*, 2005(156), 21–53. https://doi.org/10.1515/semi.2005.2005.156.21.

Heine, B. 2023. *The Grammar of Interactives*. Oxford: Oxford University Press.

Hick, W. E. 1952. On the rate of gain of information. *Quarterly Journal of Experimental Psychology*, 4(1), 11–26.

Hickmann, M. 2008. *Children's Discourse: Person, Space and Time Across Languages*. Cambridge: Cambridge University Press.

Hills, D. 2022. Metaphor. In E. Zalta & U. Nodelman (eds.), *The Stanford Encyclopedia of Philosophy* (Fall 2022 Edition), https://plato.stanford.edu/archives/fall2022/entries/metaphor/.

Hoffmann, C. & Bublitz, W. (eds). 2017. *Pragmatics of Social Media*. Berlin, Boston: De Gruyter Mouton.

Holler, J. & Levinson, S. C. 2019. Multimodal language processing in human communication. *Trends in Cognitive Sciences*, 23(8), 639–52.

Holtgraves, T. 1994. Communication in context: the effects of speaker status on the comprehension of indirect requests. *Journal of Experimental Learning, Memory and Cognition*, 20, 1205–18.

Hömke, P., Holler, J. & Levinson, S. C. 2018. Eye blinks are perceived as communicative signals in human face-to-face interaction. *PLoS One*, 13(12), e0208030. https://doi.org/10.1371/journal.pone.0208030.

Horn, L. 1972. *On the Semantic Properties of Logical Operators in English*. Doctoral dissertation, University of California at Los Angeles. Ann Arbor, MI: University Microfilms.

Horn, L. 1989. *A Natural History of Negation*. Chicago: Chicago University Press (reissued 2001 CSLI).

Huang, Y. 2007. *Pragmatics*. Oxford: Oxford University Press.

Indefrey P. & Levelt W. J. 2004. The spatial and temporal signatures of word production components. *Cognition*, 92(1–2), 101–44. https://doi.org/10.1016/j.cognition.2002.06.001.PMID:15037128.

Jaszczolt, K. 2023. *Semantics, Pragmatics, Philosophy: A Journey through Meaning*. Cambridge: Cambridge University Press

Jucker, A. & Taavitsainen, I. (eds.) 2010. *Historical Pragmatics*. Berlin, New York: De Gruyter Mouton.

Karttunen, L. & Peters, S. 1979. Conventional implicature. In C.-K. Oh & D. Dineen (eds.), *Syntax & Semantics 11: Presupposition*, New York: Academic Press, pp. 1–56

Kasirer, A. & Mashal, N. 2014. Verbal creativity in autism: Comprehension and generation of metaphoric language in high-functioning autism spectrum disorder and typical development. *Frontiers in Human Neuroscience*, 8, 615. https://doi.org/10.3389/fnhum.2014.00615.

Kendrick, K., Brown, P., Dingemanse, M. et al. 2020. Sequence organization: A universal infrastructure for social action. *Journal of Pragmatics*, 168, 119–38.

Kendrick, K. H., Holler, J. & Levinson, S. C. 2023. Turn-taking in human face-to-face interaction is multimodal: Gaze direction and manual gestures aid the coordination of turn transitions. *Philosophical Transactions of the Royal Society of London, Series B: Biological Sciences*, 378(1875), 20210473. https://doi.org/10.1098/rstb.2021.0473.

Kita, S., van Gijn, I. & van der Hulst, H. 1998. Movement phases in signs and co-speech gestures, and their transcription by human coders. In I. Wachsmuth & M. Fröhlich (eds.), *Gesture and Sign Language in Human-Computer Interaction*, Berlin: Springer, pp. 23–35.

Korta, K. & Perry, J. 2020. Pragmatics. In E. Zalta (ed.), *The Stanford Encyclopedia of Philosophy* (Spring 2020 Edition), https://plato.stanford.edu/archives/spr2020/entries/pragmatics/.

Kovecses, Z. 2005. *Metaphor in Culture: Universality and Variation*. Cambridge: Cambridge University Press.

Ladd, R. 2014. *Simultaneous Structure in Phonology*. Oxford: Oxford University Press.

Lakoff, G. & Johnson, M. 1980. *Metaphors We Live By*. Chicago: University of Chicago Press.

Lakoff, R. 1973. The logic of politeness; or, minding your P's and Q's. In C. Corum, T. Cedric Smith-Stark & A. Weiser (eds.), *Papers from the Ninth*

Regional Meeting of the Chicago Linguistics Society, Chicago: Department of Linguistics, University of Chicago, pp. 292–305.

Laver, J. 1994. *Principles of Phonetics*. Cambridge: Cambridge University Press

Leech, G. 1983. *Principles of Pragmatics*. London: Longman Group.

Levelt, W. 1989. *Speaking*. Cambridge, MA: MIT.

Levinson, S. C. 1979a. Activity types and language. *Linguistics*, 17(5/6): 356–99.

Levinson, S. C. 1979b. Pragmatics and social deixis. *Proceedings of the Fifth Annual Meeting of the Berkeley Linguistics Society*, BLS 5, 206–223.

Levinson, S. C. 1983. *Pragmatics*. Cambridge: Cambridge University Press.

Levinson, S. C. 1987. Minimization and conversational inference. In M. Bertuccelli Papi & J. Verschueren (eds.), *The Pragmatic Perspective: Selected Papers from the 1985 International Pragmatics Conference*, Amsterdam: Benjamins, pp. 61–129.

Levinson, S. C. 2000. *Presumptive Meanings*. Cambridge, MA: MIT.

Levinson, S. C. 2003. Contextualizing 'contextualization cues'. In S. Eerdmans, C. Prevignano & P. Thibault (eds.), *Language and interaction: Discussions with John J. Gumperz*, Amsterdam: John Benjamins, pp. 31–9.

Levinson, S. C. 2013a. Recursion in pragmatics. *Language*, 89, 149–62. https://doi.org/10.1353/lan.2013.0005.

Levinson, S. C. 2013b. Action formation and ascription. In T. Stivers & J. Sidnell (eds.), *The Handbook of Conversation Analysis*, Malden, MA: Wiley-Blackwell, pp. 103–30.

Levinson, S. C. 2016. Turn-taking in human communication, origins, and implications for language processing. *Trends in Cognitive Sciences*, 20(1), 6–14. https://doi.org/10.1016/j.tics.2015.10.010.

Levinson, S. C. 2019. Interactional foundations of language: The interaction engine hypothesis. In P. Hagoort (ed.), *Human Language: From Genes and Brain to Behavior*, Cambridge, MA: MIT Press, pp. 189–200.

Levinson, S. C. 2023. On cognitive artefacts. In R. Feldhay (ed.), *The Evolution of Knowledge: A Scientific Meeting in Honor of Jürgen Renn*. Berlin: Max Planck Institute for the History of Science, pp. 59–78.

Levinson, S. C. & Annamalai, E. 1992. Why presuppositions aren't conventional. In R. N. Srivastava (ed.), *Language and Text: Studies in Honour of Ashok R. Kelkar*. Dehli: Kalinga Publications, pp. 227–42. www.mpi.nl/people/levinson-stephen/publications?search_terms=annamalai.

Levinson, S. C., Cutfield, S., Dunn, M., Enfield, N. & Meira, S. (eds.) 2018. *Demonstratives in Cross-Linguistic Perspective*. Cambridge: Cambridge University Press.

Levinson S. C. & Torreira, F. 2015. Timing in turn-taking and its implications for processing models of language. *Frontiers in Psychology*, 6, 731. https://doi.org/10.3389/fpsyg.2015.00731.

Liesenfeld, A. & Dingemanse, M. 2022. Bottom-up discovery of structure and variation in response tokens ('backchannels') across diverse languages. *Proceedings of Interspeech 2022*, 1126–30. https://doi.org/10.21437/Interspeech.2022-11288.

Loos, C., German, A. & Meier, R. P. 2022. Simultaneous structures in sign languages: Acquisition and emergence. *Frontiers in Psychology*, 13, 992589. https://doi.org/10.3389/fpsyg.2022.992589.

Lyons, J. 1977. *Semantics*. Cambridge: Cambridge University Press.

Mark, D. M., Turk, A. G., Burenhult, N. & Stea, D. (eds.), 2011. *Landscape in Language: Transdisciplinary Perspectives*. Amsterdam: John Benjamins.

Meyer, A. S. 2023. Timing in conversation. *Journal of Cognition*, 6(1), 1–17. https://doi.org/10.5334/joc.268.

Ochs Keenan, E. 1976. The universality of conversational implicature. *Language in Society*, 5, 67–80.

Özyurek, A. 2014. Hearing and seeing meaning in speech and gesture: Insights from brain and behaviour. *Philosophical Transactions of the Royal Society of London, Series B: Biological Sciences*, 369(1651), 20130296. https://doi.org/10.1098/rstb.2013.0296.

Pouscoulous, N. 2011. Metaphor: For adults only? *Cognitive and Empirical Pragmatics*, 25, 51–79. https://doi.org/10.1075/BJL.25.04POU.

Pustejovsky, J. 1995. *The Generative Lexicon*. Cambridge, MA: The MIT Press.

Recanati, F. 2004. *Literal Meaning*. Cambridge: Cambridge University Press.

Rosaldo, M. 1982. The things we do with words: Ilongot speech acts and speech act theory in philosophy. *Language in Society*, 11(2), 203–37.

Rühlemann, C. 2020. Turn structure and inserts. *International Journal of Corpus Linguistics*, 252, 185–214.

Russell, J. 1995. Facial expressions of emotion: What lies beyond minimal universality? *Psychological Bulletin*, 118(3), 379–91. https://doi.org/10.1037/0033-2909.118.3.379.

Sacks, H. 1967–1972. Lecture notes. Mimeo. Later printed as *Lectures on Conversation*, G. Jefferson (ed.), 1995, Wiley-Blackwell.

Sacks, H. & Schegloff, E. 1979. Two preferences in the organization of reference to persons in conversation and their interaction. In G. Psathas (ed.), *Everyday Language: Studies in Ethnomethodology*. New York: Irvington.

(Reprinted in Enfield, N. & Stivers, T. 2009. *Person Reference in Interaction.* Cambridge: Cambridge University Press, pp. 23–9).

Schegloff, E. 1996. Confirming allusions: Toward an empirical account of action. *American Journal of Sociology,* 102(1), 161–216. https://doi.org/10.1086/230911.

Schegloff, E. 2007. *Sequential Organization in Interaction.* Cambridge: Cambridge University Press.

Schegloff, E. & Sacks, H. 1973. Opening Up Closings. *Semiotica,* 7(4), 289–327.

Searle, J. 1969. *Speech Acts.* Cambridge: Cambridge University Press.

Senft, G. 2008. The case: The Trobriand Islanders vs H.P. Grice. Kilivila and the Gricean maxims of quality and manner. *Anthropos,* 103, 139–47.

Senft, G. 2014. *Understanding Pragmatics: An Interdisciplinary Approach to Language Use.* Abingdon: Routledge.

Shannon, C. E. & Weaver, W. 1949. *The Mathematical Theory of Communication.* University of Illinois Press.

Skirgård, H., Haynie, H., Blasi, D. et al. 2023. Grambank reveals the importance of genealogical constraints on linguistic diversity and highlights the impact of language loss. *Science Advances,* 9, eadg6175. https://doi.org/10.1126/sciadv.adg6175.

Song, Y. 2020. Simile and metaphor interpretation in children. *English Language Teaching,* 13(4): 91–103.

Sperber, D. & Wilson, D. 1986. *Relevance.* Oxford: Blackwell.

Stalnaker, R. 1974. Pragmatic presuppositions. In M. Munitz & P. Unger (eds.), *Semantics & Philosophy,* New York: NYU Press, pp. 135–47.

Stivers, T., Enfield, N. J., Brown, P. et al. 2009. Universals and cultural variation in turn-taking in conversation. *Proceedings of the National Academy of Sciences,* 106(26), 10587–92.

Strauss, C. 2004. Cultural standing in expression of opinion. *Language in Society,* 33(2), 161–94.

Strawson, P. 1950. On referring. *Mind,* 59, 320–44.

Tomasello, M. 2008. *Origins of Human Communication.* Cambridge, MA: MIT Press.

Wilbur R. B. 2009. Effects of varying rate of signing on ASL manual signs and nonmanual markers. *Lang Speech,* 52(Pt 2–3):245–85.

Wilson, D. & Sperber, D. 2004. Relevance theory. In L. Horn & G. Ward (eds.), *The Handbook of Pragmatics,* Oxford: Blackwell, pp. 607–632.

Wright, R., Mansfield, C. & Panfili, L. 2019. Voice quality types and uses in North American English. *Anglophonia,* 27. https://doi.org/10.4000/anglophonia.1952.

Yang, Y. 2019. *The Management of Topics in Ordinary Conversation.* PhD University of York, Language and Linguistic Science, September 2019.

Zipf, G. K. 1949. *Human Behavior and the Principle of Least Effort.* Cambridge, MA: Addison-Wesley.

Acknowledgements

This Element is based on the Presidential address to the International Pragmatics Conference, Brussels, July 2023. I am grateful to the audience for comments and encouragement. My thanks to Michael Haugh for suggesting this mode of publication, and to Jay Atlas, Penelope Brown, Dan Dediu, Mark Dingemanse, Ad Foolen, Antje Meyer and Tanya Freedman for comments on a draft. The editors of the series, Michael Haugh and Jonathan Culpeper, both provided helpful feedback.

Cambridge Elements ☰

Pragmatics

Jonathan Culpeper
Lancaster University, UK

Jonathan Culpeper is Professor of English Language and Linguistics in the Department of Linguistics and English Language at Lancaster University, UK. A former co-editor-in-chief of the *Journal of Pragmatics* (2009–14), with research spanning multiple areas within pragmatics, his major publications include: *Impoliteness: Using Language to Cause Offence* (2011, CUP) and *Pragmatics and the English Language* (2014, Palgrave; with Michael Haugh).

Michael Haugh
University of Queensland, Australia

Michael Haugh is Professor of Linguistics and Applied Linguistics in the School of Languages and Cultures at the University of Queensland, Australia. A former co-editor-in-chief of the *Journal of Pragmatics* (2015–2020), with research spanning multiple areas within pragmatics, his major publications include: *Understanding Politeness* (2013, CUP; with Dániel Kádár), *Pragmatics and the English Language* (2014, Palgrave; with Jonathan Culpeper), and *Im/politeness Implicatures* (2015, Mouton de Gruyter).

Advisory Board

About the Series

The Cambridge Elements in Pragmatics series showcases dynamic and high-quality original, concise and accessible scholarly works. Written for a broad pragmatics readership it encourages dialogue across different perspectives on language use. It is a forum for cutting-edge work in pragmatics: consolidating theory (especially through cross-fertilization), leading the development of new methods, and advancing innovative topics in pragmatics.

Cambridge Elements ☰

Pragmatics

www.ingramcontent.com/pod-product-compliance
Ingram Content Group UK Ltd.
Pitfield, Milton Keynes, MK11 3LW, UK
UKHW021041090225
454697UK00029BA/85